D0771001

Scale 1:40 000 000; one inch to 630 miles. Lambert's Azimuthal, Equal Area Projection
Elevations and depressions are given in feet

*Enchantment of the World*

# VIETNAM

*By David K. Wright*

**Consultant for Vietnam:** Clark D. Neher, Ph.D., Chairman, Department of Political Science, Northern Illinois University, DeKalb, Illinois

**Consultant for Reading:** Robert L. Hillerich, Ph.D., Bowling Green State University, Bowling Green, Ohio

CHILDRENS PRESS ®

CHICAGO

*Produce being carried to market in a traditional manner*

## Picture Acknowledgments

© **Superstock:** 4, 10 (2 photos), 19 (top left & middle right), 20 (2 photos), 48 (left), 84 (left), 85, 88 (top), 104, 107 (bottom left & right)

**AP/Wide World Photos:** 5, 29 (2 photos), 31, 33, 35 (2 photos), 36, 38, 45 (2 photos), 55 (2 photos), 57 (3 photos), 59 (2 photos), 64 (left), 77 (right), 78, 79 (right)

**Root Resources:** © John Chitty: 6, 47, 50, 62 (bottom), 64 (right), 66 (top), 77 (left), 83 (left); © Alan G. Nelson: 19 (bottom left); © Jane P. Downton: 102 (right)

**Shostal Associates, Inc.:** 39, (right), 100 (inset), 103 (left); © Joe Smoljan: Cover, 8, 9, 19 (top right), 43, 48 (right), 65, 66 (bottom left & right), 71 (middle & right), 73 (left), 80, 88 (bottom), 91, 92, 93, 100, 103 (right), 106, 107 (top), 108 (bottom), 109, 110 (3 photos), 111, 114, 122

© **Photri:** 14 (bottom), 17, 39 (left), 62 (top), 68, 70 (right), 72 (right), 73 (right), 74, 79 (left), 83 (right), 84 (right), 94 (2 photos), 102 (left), 105 (2 photos): © Lance Downing: 12 (2 photos); © B. Kulik: 14 (top), 22, 60 (right), 69 (right), 108 (top)

**Third Coast Stock Source:** © Tim Waite: 16, 69 (left), 70 (left), 71 (left), 72 (left), 75, 79 (middle)

**Historical Pictures Service, Chicago:** 25, 26 (2 photos), 27 (2 photos)

**Journalism Services:** © Jim Bryant: 60 (left)

**Len W. Meents:** Maps on pages 101, 104, 106, 109

**Courtesy Flag Research Center, Winchester, Massachusetts 01890:** Flag on back cover

**Cover:** Ho Chi Minh City

Library of Congress Cataloging-in-Publication Data

Wright, David K.
    Vietnam / by David K. Wright.
        p.    cm. — (Enchantment of the world)
    Includes index.
    Summary: Discusses the geography, history, people, economy, and customs of Vietnam.
    ISBN 0-516-02712-3
    1.   Vietnam—Juvenile
literature.  [1.   Vietnam.]   I.   Title.   II.   Series.
DS556.3.W75   1989                        88-30486
959.7—dc19                                     CIP
                                               AC

*A new generation of Vietnamese in western dress*

## TABLE OF CONTENTS

*The French built tea plantations in the fertile mountain areas.*

# Chapter 1

# A COMPLEX COUNTRY

Clouds of conflict have for centuries hung over the country we call Vietnam. That is because Vietnam is near one of the great crossroads on our planet. It is a small land between the huge nations of China and India. In fact, one historic name for this Southeast Asia area is Indochina. The Vietnamese themselves are a mixture of Chinese and Indonesian people.

## A SUBTROPICAL LAND

The Socialist Republic of Vietnam is a long, thin country above the equator, with a subtropical climate. It is about 1,030 miles (1,657 kilometers) from north to south, but as few as 50 miles (80 kilometers) from east to west at its narrowest point. Northern Vietnam is cool and wet in the winter; the south is sometimes wet and always hot. Vietnam's northern neighbor is China. To the west are the countries of Laos and Cambodia (officially called Kampuchea). East are the Gulf of Tonkin and the South China Sea. South is the Gulf of Thailand. These seas are part of the western edge of the Pacific Ocean.

The Vietnamese sometimes think of their country as a pole with a basket of rice on each end. That's very accurate, since wide river

*The Hai Van pass near Da Nang*

deltas in the north and south make conditions ideal for growing rice. Even when the recent war was at its height, the country remained one of the world's leading rice producers.

## TOPOGRAPHY

The two large river deltas are wide and very low. In fact, dikes have been built to keep the sea from turning rich, rice-paddy farms into salty, useless swamp. A thin line of jungle-covered mountains runs from north to south. The mountains are called the Annamites. The very highest mountains, far to the north near China, extend over 10,000 feet (3,048 meters). Most of the country is thick with vegetation. That includes narrow coastal lands, where farmers grow crops in poor soil. The country has several natural harbors used as ports for oceangoing ships.

*Poling a boat through a rice paddy*

Rice is the major food for all of the people who live in Vietnam. That includes the soldier guarding the Chinese border, who carries rice in his cloth sling. It includes a mountain-dwelling mother, who is so isolated that she has never seen a car, and the schoolchild, who lives in a major city such as Ho Chi Minh City (formerly Saigon).

## THE PEOPLE

Many different kinds of people can be found in this country. About 85 percent are the people we think of as Vietnamese. They live along the coast and in the rich river deltas. Far to the south, in the Mekong River Delta, there are numerous Cambodians. In the hilly central highlands live dozens of tribes that look like each other, but do not resemble the Vietnamese. Their tribal names

*A Catholic church (left) and the interior of a Buddhist temple (right)*

include Rhade, Hmong, and Tai. A few Vietnamese of Chinese descent can be found in Ho Chi Minh City, where the suburb of Cholon is almost all Chinese.

There are at least as many religions as there are kinds of people. Most Vietnamese are Buddhists, influenced by the Chinese religion-philosophies of Confucianism and Taoism. There are about four million Roman Catholics and several thousand other Christians. A few Muslims, followers of the Islamic religion, can be found far to the south near Cambodia. There are dozens of religions among the hill tribes. The most unusual beliefs of all may be held by the Cao Dai sect. This religion began in Vietnam in 1919 and is an attempt to blend the best of all world religions. Among its saints are the famous French writer Victor Hugo and movie comedian Charlie Chaplin.

There are other things about Vietnam and the Vietnamese that a foreigner might find puzzling. It may be a backward country economically, but the Vietnamese are complex and there are many ancient rules that tell people how they should conduct their lives.

# TWO COUNTRIES BECOME ONE

Since 1975, Vietnam has been one country again. The thirty-six provinces were united after thirty years of war that cost 1.3 million lives and billions of dollars. Today the country is 127,242 square miles (329,556 square kilometers). It is about the size of Italy or the state of New Mexico and is made up of the former countries of North Vietnam and South Vietnam.

The government has imposed communism on the country. The Communists were North Vietnamese and certain South Vietnamese who fought the southern government as secret, or guerrilla, troops called the *Viet Cong* (VC). The goal of both sets of forces was to reunite the country. They believed that a decision made in 1954 to split Vietnam temporarily into two countries was unfair. It had been forced upon the people, they said.

The new Communist government at first issued many orders to the people. Farmers who owned even tiny plots of land were told that it would be taken and divided equally among everyone. Merchants were ordered to shut stores and factories if they did not turn over all profits to the government. The results were a disaster. Crop yields dropped, necessities such as cloth and household items disappeared, and the country suffered near starvation and an economic tailspin.

Today, there appears to be some optimism. The good feeling is due to the fact that small shopkeepers recently have been allowed to work independently. Small landowners grow whatever crops work best and provide enough for their families. Many "reeducation camps," where stubborn farmers and small businessmen were sent, are closed now or almost empty.

*Boats crowded with refugees left Vietnam after the war.*

## POSTWAR SUFFERING

Sadly, many people suffered between the end of the war and today. Those who suffered most were officials and military officers of the old South Vietnamese government. Many were killed or put in prisons. Their families were refused food. Persons of Chinese descent, never trusted by the Vietnamese, were encouraged to leave the country in old, unsafe boats.

Ethnic Chinese and Vietnamese who were considered enemies of the new government became known to the world as boat people. Until world opinion forced the Vietnamese to stop sending these people to their deaths at sea, the government actually made money by demanding payment so that people could leave. Thousands left beginning in 1978. Many of them drowned, starved to death, or died of disease on the vast ocean.

The government also has troubles from outside the country. The Chinese launched an attack across Vietnam's northern border in 1979. The reason for the invasion was the late 1978 attack on

Cambodia by the Vietnamese. All three nations have Communist governments, but that does not mean that they like or trust each other. The Vietnamese have always feared the Chinese nation, even though much Vietnamese culture comes from China. Today, these neighbors stare at each other across a heavily armed border.

Vietnam has other worries. A major concern is the poverty and need of its people. Because the government has many enemies, it gets little aid and is not trusted by more prosperous nations. The Soviet Union and Japan trade with Vietnam. But debts with these two countries continue to pile up. Soviets now occupy United States bases built more than twenty years ago.

With a population of about sixty-two million people, Vietnam may have to expand. To relieve urban overcrowding and unemployment, thousands of its citizens have been moved to farmland in rural Vietnam. However, many citizens have been opposed to this displacement.

There is no indication that Vietnamese soldiers will soon leave Cambodia or Laos. Together, these two neighbors have fewer than nine million people. Cambodia is a food producer and Laos has unexplored mineral deposits. It is possible that Vietnamese civilians will eventually settle in the two neighboring lands.

Like most nations, there is some cause for optimism among the Vietnamese. Their country today is poor, but it has a powerful army. No country in Southeast Asia—Burma, Cambodia, Indonesia, Laos, Malaysia, Singapore, Thailand, or the Philippines—would dare attack it. This creates a sense of pride in the people, but they are aware that supporting a huge army prevents them from advancing in other areas. And they realize that they continue to live in the shadow of China, a huge and sometimes unpredictable neighbor.

The seacoast at Nha Trang (above) and a majestic waterfall in the highland area (below)

# Chapter 2

# *WATER, WATER EVERYWHERE*

Water is plentiful in Vietnam. The country's east coast is formed by warm and usually calm ocean water. The long rivers, the Red in the north and the Mekong in the south, are major highways. Off these large rivers are smaller rivers and canals that allow the Vietnamese a means of travel. Water is important even where there are no rivers, since the annual monsoon rains allow jungle to grow even where soils are poor.

Monsoons are great, seasonal winds that sweep across south Asia, traveling northeast half the year and southwest the other half. These winds make the north rainy and cool in the winter and warm in the summer. They cause rain showers so regularly in parts of the country that people can step inside at the same time every day for weeks and stay dry. In months when there is no rain, there is so much surface water that no one misses the falling rain. An American soldier said, "It's the only place I've ever been where you can be standing up to your knees in water, with dust blowing in your face."

*A taxicab tries to get through the flooding water in the monsoon season.*

## TYPHOONS CAN STRIKE

Occasionally, a typhoon (a tropical hurricane) will strike. This severe storm uproots trees, knocks down homes, and causes coastal flooding. Floods occur on a regular and expected basis in Vietnam, where people take advantage of them to fill farm ponds and rice paddies. The two rivers have created low-lying, broad farming areas. Dikes, especially in the north, keep the salty high tide from killing crops. Remarkably, high tides affect the Mekong River for about 300 miles (483 kilometers). That's as far inland as Phnom Penh, the capital of Cambodia.

The southern tip of Vietnam is just eight degrees north of the equator. The northern edge is very near the Tropic of Cancer. Ho Chi Minh City has a steamy average annual temperature of 81 degrees Fahrenheit (27.2 degrees Celsius) and Hanoi, the capital, averages 74 degrees Fahrenheit (23.3 degrees Celsius). Relief from the heat can be found at higher elevations. The southern hill city of Da Lat, for example, is 4,920 feet (1,500 meters) above sea level. The average annual temperature is 70 degrees Fahrenheit (21.1 degrees Celsius).

*Rice paddies in the Mekong River delta*

Water, warmth, and good ground are needed to grow things.
The best growing areas are the floodplains or deltas. The topsoil
from upriver is deposited there. That soil has drained off the
mountains, leaving rocky, poor ground behind. The Red River got
its name from the red soil it carries. The Mekong River carries
much better soil and is responsible for most of the rice crop.

Between the deltas, the coast is narrow. To the west of the coast
are hills and mountains. In the north, the mountains are covered
with evergreens and valuable hardwoods such as teak. Parts of the
central and south feature dense jungle that allows no direct sun to
strike the forest floor. Much of the forest was destroyed during the
Vietnam War when herbicides were dropped from war planes.
There also are large areas of bamboo, grass, and mangrove, a
knotty, short tree that grows along the coast and near other
waterways.

Despite more than thirty years oi war, there are many animals in the forests. The largest wild animal is the elephant, slightly smaller than the African elephant and very intelligent and easy to train if caught. Soldiers sometimes rode elephants into the fighting during wars, despite protests from the owners, who used the beasts to pull fallen logs out of the jungles. Once in a while, a herd of elephants will look almost red. These animals have been cooling off in the northern soil, which covers their leathery, gray hides.

There also are wild oxen, wild pigs, piglike tapirs, deer that bark like dogs and give off a musty smell, leopards and a variety of other wildcats, black and honey bears, skunks, squirrels, otters, mongeese, and, of course, mice and rats. The rat is everywhere. In the central highlands, rats are trapped and roasted for eating.

Water-dwelling creatures range in size from the crocodile to the tiny leech. This creature, at home in or out of water, attaches itself silently to exposed human or animal skin. It sucks blood for its nourishment before falling off and leaving an itchy, swollen bite. Water is where mosquitoes breed. These insects seem to bite all of the time and carry malaria, a tropical disease that causes chills, fever, and sweating. Flies are everywhere.

Unpleasant insects and other harmful creatures seem right at home in Vietnam. Beetles that vary in size from a pinhead to a matchbox always seem to turn up in stored foods such as grain or flour. Scorpions are large, black or brown insectlike creatures with curved tails that contain poisonous stingers. Poisonous snakes are common on land and sea, but for sheer size, the python is the snake most apt to draw everyone's attention. These snakes can

*Some animals in Vietnam, clockwise from top left: a python, a monkey, a wild ox, and an elephant*

grow to thirty feet (nine meters) and weigh several hundred pounds. They squeeze and then swallow whole good-sized animals. A chicken, for example, can be eaten in one bite by a hungry python.

There have been 586 different kinds of birds identified in southern Vietnam alone. Thick jungles hum with insects and sing with birds that may show flashes of brilliant orange, blue, or green feathers as they fly. Monkeys cavort in the treetops, too. They can be tiny rhesus monkeys, the kind commonly used in biological experiments, or more exotic langurs, macaques, and gibbons. Monkeys serve some Vietnamese as pets and others as food.

The Vietnamese enjoy fish and are skilled at catching and preparing them. Several recipes include soft-shelled crab. Lobsters

*Sampans (left) and the My Tho Flower Market in the Mekong Delta (right)*

are common near the southern coast. *Sampans*—small boats not much bigger than rowboats—haul in saltwater squids, octopus, and shrimp, plus more conventional fish. Fishermen who fled Vietnam after the war have found work along the United States Gulf coast. Their skills are respected, though American fishermen fear the Vietnamese will overfish local beds.

## PLANT LIFE ABOUNDS

The weather is so inviting in parts of Vietnam that flowers can be grown for shipment all over the world. Orchids are imported by florists from beds around the city of Da Lat. Other domesticated plants include the short, thin rubber tree and bushes where tea leaves flourish. Banana, guava, papaya, and coconut trees also produce well here.

With warm weather all the time, trees, shrubs, and plants bloom and lose their leaves in different months. These leaves are important for tropical plants, because these old leaves are sometimes the only predictable source of nourishment for the soil. Plants that show the most economic potential for the Vietnamese are the many varieties of hardwoods. These woods make beautiful and very strong furniture. Mahogany and teak, the two most popular, are prized all over the world. But roads will have to improve before these trees can be brought to market in large quantities.

## NATURAL RESOURCES

Fuel may be one of Vietnam's major resources. Coal is commonly mined near Hanoi, while offshore oil deposits show quite a bit of promise. Phosphate, which is an important ingredient in fertilizer, is plentiful. Also mined are chromite, tin, antimony, bauxite, gold, iron ore, lead, tungsten, zinc, and lime. There are fewer resources in southern Vietnam.

## FUTURE PROSPECTS

Phosphate, a key fertilizer, is plentiful. There is enough for export and for use on new, quick-growing rice seeds. That means Vietnamese should be able to feed themselves for the next several decades. Oil is probably present in offshore seabeds, but the quantity is not known. The Soviets and several other countries have been looking for oil for a decade. A large deposit of oil could help Vietnam greatly, even though world prices are at present not very high.

*The eight-hundred-year-old Cham Temple*

# Chapter 3
# CONQUERING
## A RUGGED LAND

No one is sure where the Vietnamese originated. They may be from southern China, or the Red River valley area of northern Vietnam. The very first residents of present-day Vietnam were Negroid pygmies. They were followed by Negritos, who are no longer in the country but who left a few characteristics among the people of today who dwell in the Annamite Mountains.

Around 1500 B.C., Indonesians arrived from the south and moved as far north as modern China. The very first kingdom, named Champa, was founded on Vietnam's east coast. This kingdom later was influenced by Indian explorers. Traces of these early people can be seen today in the few remaining Cham people of central Vietnam. Various people—Thais, Chinese, and Indonesians—mixed to create the distinct Vietnamese people around the time of the birth of Christ.

The Vietnamese learned their language from the Indonesians and Thais, but they learned much more from the advanced Chinese. Government, literature, philosophy, and technical matters were absorbed from China. Cultural habits have come from all parts of southeast Asia and can be seen today in highland regions and in such adornments as tattoos and jewelry. These and other cultural matters kept the Vietnamese distinctive from the Chinese, who soon conquered their small country.

China ruled Vietnam for one thousand years. During that time (100 B.C.-A.D. 900), Vietnamese occasionally rebelled. But they were able to become a separate country only by pledging loyalty to mighty China. The first Europeans arrived about 1500. They were Portuguese, who were wonderful sailors, but very poor at getting along with people in a foreign land. For about one hundred years, the Portuguese traded weapons and various trinkets with the Vietnamese, for pepper and spices, gems, and cloth, which they brought back to Europe.

The French established a small colony on the east coast of India in the 1600s. They conducted some trade with Vietnam, but the Vietnamese disliked foreigners. So the French departed. But they left Roman Catholic missionaries who tried to better the peasants as they taught Christianity. The priests introduced the written alphabet, still used today. They converted many Vietnamese, then took the side of local Christians in battles for control of parts of the country.

For hundreds of years, the missionaries were never sure of their position. During the reign of one ruler, they would be important members of his court. During the reign of the next ruler, they might fear for their lives. Vietnamese who thought Confucianism was good, believed Christianity was bad. By 1843, the French returned to Southeast Asia in force. They said they were there to protect Christians, but they wanted land to rule.

After several years of expensive military campaigns that did not work, the French attacked Saigon in 1861. The French quickly

*The French capture the citadel of Saigon in 1859.*

took the city and were given three nearby provinces and an island. This allowed the French to control the rice crop and they were able to starve Vietnamese rebels into giving up. Resistance spread among villagers throughout the country. So the French decided to take more territory. In 1874, Vietnamese Emperor Tu Duc signed a treaty that gave France all of Vietnam. In exchange, the French promised to protect Tu Duc and his people from outside forces. In view of the way the French treated the Vietnamese, outside forces might have been a welcome change.

When the French took control, 80 percent of all Vietnamese could read. When they left seventy years later, only 20 percent of the Vietnamese were able to read. While the French got rich from large plantations, the Vietnamese were forced to work long hours in low-paying jobs. Even worse for the natives, who value self-respect, the French made the Vietnamese feel inferior.

Frenchmen did not escape unharmed from this new and unfamiliar country. Malaria, dysentery, tuberculosis, typhoid, and

*The French attack a fort on the Saigon River (top)
and the citadel of Saigon (above).*

other diseases killed hundreds of French soldiers. The heat also produced casualties as the heavily armed Europeans slogged through rice paddies where daytime temperatures exceeded 100 degrees Fahrenheit (37.8 degrees Celsius). In fact, for every French soldier who died in battle, twenty died from disease. A tiny cut could result in infection and amputation or death in the sticky, tropical climate.

By 1887, France controlled all of Vietnam, plus Cambodia and Laos. The French and a few Vietnamese they trained ran the country. The local people sometimes tried to rebel, but they were starved to death or attacked with guns. Even worse, the French began growing opium as a cash crop. Hundreds of Vietnamese and thousands of outsiders became addicted to the poppy by-product. Already underpaid and hungry, the Vietnamese often

*A room where processed opium was stored (left) and a fleet
on the Ganges River delivering opium to Calcutta, India (right)*

used opium or milder narcotics such as betel nuts to help forget
their stomach pains.

## THE RISE OF NATIONALISM

Due in large part to the mistreatment by the French, Vietnamese
became very nationalistic. They sought a country where the
people who were born there could make their own rules. The very
first rebellion against the French took place even before the
country was totally under French rule. Buddhist monks led
believers in a series of raids in rural areas of the southern Mekong
Delta. No sooner had the French put down the Buddhists than
another revolt erupted farther north. Bandits, pirates, and simple
farmers fought the French off and on until the Europeans left in
1954.

# HO CHI MINH

It is impossible to separate Ho Chi Minh from the events that were taking place in Vietnam. He and the people who went to school in central Vietnam in about 1900 were well educated and from the start used the teaching provided by the French to study revolution. One small French-language school in the old capital of Hue produced dozens of nationalists. Ho was the most famous.

He and fellow students saw their neighbors and parents forced to serve the French—and a few pro-French Vietnamese—just as farm animals serve the farmer. Ho left the country while still in his teens, perhaps because he realized that there was no immediate hope of battling the French. Those left behind continued to challenge the French and spent time in jail for their efforts.

Meanwhile, the Japanese were flexing their muscles. They told many Asians that it was time to throw out European influence. The Japanese attacked China in 1937 and, because China was split apart even before the Japanese came, used the huge country for target practice. The French in Vietnam saw what was happening and could do little but worry. By the time the Japanese threatened Vietnam, France had been overrun by the Germans and World War II had begun.

The French left in charge were ordered to cooperate with the Japanese. The Vietnamese welcomed the Japanese, but were treated as badly by them as they had been treated by the French. Was there no hope for freedom, they wondered. The Japanese told them what crops to raise and did not permit the farmers to keep enough to live. Hundreds of thousands died of starvation as the goods they produced helped feed Japanese soldiers.

*Occupying Japanese troops (left) enter Indochina in 1941. Ho Chi Mihn in 1950 (right)*

Throughout World War II, small bands of Vietnamese worked with the United States and other Allied forces to make life unpleasant for the Japanese. The Americans were soldiers and pilots who had to transport arms to Chinese fighting the Japanese. These United States troops sometimes were shot down over Vietnam. Vietnamese braved packs of Japanese soldiers in order to rescue and hide the downed Americans. These rescues started cooperation between the Vietnamese and the Allies. Surplus weapons and supplies were given to the small men who somehow survived in thick jungles and on rocky slopes.

Ho Chi Minh, back in Vietnam, battled malaria and the Japanese. He became the leader of the Vietnamese Communist party and the person many patriotic Vietnamese looked to for leadership when the war ended. As the Japanese prepared to surrender, starving peasants all across the country attacked them with hoes, knives, and clubs. The Japanese—and the French—feared going into many parts of the country. Meanwhile, Ho Chi Minh and his supporters entered Hanoi and declared Vietnam independent.

# WAR WITH THE FRENCH

France decided to return to Vietnam as a colonial power in 1946. They had not taken seriously Ho Chi Minh's declaration of independence, even though he had copied many of the phrases from America's revolution against the British in the eighteenth century. In fact, the British under Winston Churchill said they felt it was all right for the French to rule Vietnam. Franklin Roosevelt disagreed, but the American president died before World War II ended. The French returned and were faced with a hostile population.

Earlier, Ho Chi Minh had attempted to be granted independence by the French. But they had tricked him, he believed. Some of Ho's backers complained that he would even deal with the French. But Ho pointed out that allowing the French to return was at least better then having the Chinese back as overlords. The French, Ho said, were tired of war and would not put up much of a fight to keep Indochina. But the Chinese would move in and not leave for one thousand years, just as they had done in the past.

Communist soldiers drifted into the main northern cities of Hanoi and Haiphong. There was an uneasy cease-fire between them and the French. But it was soon broken. French troops demanded that the guerrilla fighters withdraw from the port of Haiphong. Before the Vietnamese could answer this demand, French tanks and artillery were used and a battleship sailed into the port. The ship shelled areas of the city where the Vietnamese soldiers were camped. Historians feel this marked the start of the war between the French and the Vietnamese.

Earlier, far to the south, the United States had sent a few military men to look after Allied prisoners of war. The Americans

*French North African troops on the outskirts of Hanoi*

failed to get along with the British or the French and did not have much success in locating Americans they thought were being held captive. One American, Peter Dewey of Chicago, was killed by Communist guerrillas when they mistook him for a Frenchman. Dewey was the first of what were to be almost sixty thousand United States fatalities in Southeast Asia.

Other innocent people were dying in French Indochina. A group of French soldiers, who had been arrested by the Japanese, were released in Saigon and went on a rampage. They were joined by angry French civilians. This mob broke into numerous homes of innocent Vietnamese and killed men, women, and children. At about the same time, a gang of Communists and terrorists kidnapped more than one hundred European children. Many were killed and others were mutilated. These were terrible hints of things to come.

# Chapter 4

# *THE FRENCH DEPART, THE AMERICANS ARRIVE*

---

The French wanted to hold on to Vietnam after World War II. Ho Chi Minh believed that if the Vietnamese put down their weapons, they would never be free of outside rulers. So Ho and his guerrilla military leader, Vo Nguyen Giap, recruited soldiers and headed back into the hills. They promised a future where the people would run the country. The French made no such promise.

Instead, French authorities in Vietnam found a young man whose ancestors were Vietnamese kings and queens. They put this person, who was easy to order around, on a throne in the old capital of Hue. His name was Bao Dai. He was raised in France and loved to have parties and go to the movies. He signed an agreement in 1949 that said Vietnam was free and under his control. But the country's economy and military were still run by the French. Bao Dai was the head of a puppet government.

## AMERICAN AID ARRIVES

The French asked the United States for military aid to fight the guerrillas. The United States was undergoing a "red scare" at the

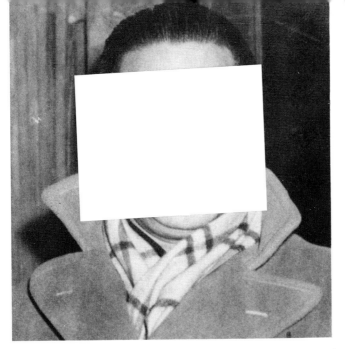

*The French installed Bao Dai as the head of a puppet government.*

time—everyone feared communism. So even though the United States was fighting in Korea, the French were quickly sent cargo planes, weapons, and supplies.

The French thought they were facing a few guerrillas with little support. They were wrong. Farmers and shopkeepers who had been angered and abused for years backed the Communists, who were called the Vietminh. Still, a few Vietnamese fought for the French. They were the small number of middle-class Vietnamese who had prospered by working for and with the French. They were Roman Catholic, usually from the north and had frequently attended French schools in France or Vietnam. They did not trust Ho Chi Minh. Many of the people who ran the government of South Vietnam from 1954 to 1975 were originally pro-French northerners.

## STREET WITHOUT JOY

French forces might have won under better conditions. Many were battle-hardened French Foreign Legionnaires from Africa and Europe. They had modern weapons, decent clothing, good food, and modern medicine. But the rugged landscape proved to be as harmful as enemy soldiers. Diseases struck the French, who sat in a string of isolated forts as monsoon rain and tropical sun beat down. Roads were narrow and cut through thick jungle that hid the enemy. One road, Route 4, became known as the Street Without Joy. Each time a French military unit used the highway, it would be ambushed. Units sent to the rescue would be ambushed, too. Life by life, the Vietminh were beating the French.

The number of Vietminh soon exceeded the number of French. The Chinese began to supply the guerrillas with modern weapons. Artillery pieces, machine guns, rifles, and ammunition captured in Korea were given to the Vietminh. Well-armed, the Communists foolishly tried to fight the French in conventional battles. They were badly beaten near Hanoi, Haiphong, and elsewhere. So they returned to hit-and-run guerrilla tactics. Gradually, the French were worn down.

## DIEN BIEN PHU

A French general named Henri Navarre came up with a plan to turn the war around. He wanted to establish a point far into northern Vietnam from which he could launch major attacks. Navarre sent his soldiers into a narrow valley near the Laotian border named Dien Bien Phu. The Vietminh immediately began to surround the French paratroopers and legionnaires. Moving by night, they hauled artillery into the mountains all around the outnumbered French.

The only way to resupply French forces was by air. But the enemy used antiaircraft fire to shoot down planes. Due to the weather, French supplies sometimes were dropped into Vietminh

*The Battle of Dien Bien Phu ended in a crushing defeat for the French.*

positions. The French officer in charge of artillery predicted that
his guns would win the battle. When the big guns were captured,
the officer killed himself.

The Vietnamese began to dig trenches toward French lines.
Wounded French soldiers could hear the digging as they lay in
damp underground shelves. Survivors tell of the terrible sound of
digging that went on all around them. They could see no one, so
there was no one to shoot—but the Vietminh shoveled ever closer.

The outnumbered French forces fought bravely—with bayonets
or their bare hands when they ran out of ammunition. Their
surrender came on May 7, 1954. Nine thousand French troops
died and more than one thousand later died or were killed while
prisoners. An even greater number of Vietminh died in and
around Dien Bien Phu. They were the victims of artillery rounds
and bombs dropped by old French planes through the fog and
mists of a northern winter and spring.

*Ngo Dinh Diem was elected prime minister in 1956.*

## ONE COUNTRY DIVIDED INTO TWO

The French agreed to withdraw their troops south of a line drawn across the middle of the country. That line, the 17th parallel, was established as a temporary border between two countries in order to separate French troops from the Vietminh. The Vietminh stayed in the north to form North Vietnam, with Hanoi as the capital. Pro-French Vietnamese went south to form South Vietnam, with the capital in Saigon.

An election was set for both countries in July 1956. Voters would decide if they wanted two countries or one, and who their leaders would be. Bao Dai, the ruler who had been put on the throne by the French, moved to France. He named an anti-Communist, Ngo Dinh Diem, as prime minister of South Vietnam. Diem then held an election and defeated the absent Bao Dai to take control of the south.

Meanwhile, in North Vietnam, anyone who owned even a tiny plot of land was in danger of losing his or her life. The government began to divide up farmland among landless peasants. Everyone who wanted to farm could have at least a small field or paddy. People who were landlords often were killed and their families chased away to starve. More than one million Vietnamese, most of them Catholic, fled south. Some of the ships provided for their transportation were furnished by the United States.

In the south, Diem took on several different groups, from the politically          Dai religious sect to the Binh Xuyen. The
n·                 g of powerful drug smugglers. They had
                   ars, sometimes with French blessing.
                   rty thousand Binh Xuyen battled for
                   s troops won and the defeated gangsters
                   a to join up with Communist guerrillas.

## A STRANGE RULER

Ngo Dinh Diem was from a Catholic family in central Vietnam. He was a well-educated bachelor who became a fierce anti-Communist and served as South Vietnam's prime minister from 1954 to 1963. He was advised by his brother, Ngo Dinh Nhu, who was head of Diem's secret police. His wife, Madame Nhu, tried to establish high morals and strict rules in Saigon. All three disliked Buddhism and may have believed that anyone who was not Catholic was a Communist.

While North Vietnam was being industrialized with help from China and the Soviets, the United States began to provide aid for South Vietnam. So many southerners opposed Diem's policies that he called off the 1956 elections that might have unified the country. Diem feared that Ho Chi Minh would win the election. This infuriated everyone in the north and many southerners. The South Vietnamese were promised peaceful land reform by Diem,

*Soldiers patrolling the streets in 1955, looking for anti-Diem forces.*

but nothing happened. The rice-rich Mekong Delta became a hideout for anti-Diem forces that ranged from gangsters to religious leaders to Communists.

South Vietnamese Communists, called Viet Cong, began to actively oppose Diem all across the country in 1957. Without warning, a car bomb would explode in Saigon, an outpost would be attacked in the Mekong Delta, or a jeep filled with government soldiers would hit a mine and blow up. The Viet Cong were getting weapons from the north, where a 1,000-mile (1,609-kilometer) path, later nicknamed the Ho Chi Minh Trail, was being used. The trail began in North Vietnam, swerved southwest into Laos, then headed south. It split in two where Vietnam, Cambodia, and Laos borders meet. One path went east toward Saigon. The other continued south into the delta. Down this primitive trail came guns, ammunition, weapons, mines, mortars, and other essentials for guerrilla warfare.

The guerrillas by day were farmers or laborers. But by night they were enemy soldiers, sniping at government buildings or planting mines or bombs. They were advised by full-time Viet

*An American soldier searching for Vietcong in a tunnel dug under a house in Saigon (left). An American officer training a Vietnamese soldier (right).*

Cong members called cadre. These people were committed to revolution and recruited soldiers in villages. Recruiting was easy; villagers felt they had no voice in the Diem government. They believed that Diem, who was not of their religion, was a puppet of foreign interests. The villagers were promised land, power, and respect if the Viet Cong won.

The United States wanted a success story in Southeast Asia, where communism threatened many emerging nations. So American officials provided Diem with money, food, supplies, weapons, equipment, and advisers. Some United States advisers were also soldiers. They trained the South Vietnamese to be soldiers, sailors, and airmen. They also taught peasants how to fortify their villages. The problem was, the peasants were sometimes forced to move to safe villages miles from their ancestral land. Many of the young people in these so-called strategic hamlets or villages joined the Viet Cong or became collaborators.

Despite their corruption and neglectful attitude toward the

people, the soldiers of South Vietnam were wearing down the lightly armed Viet Cong. The Viet Cong had to rely more and more on assassinations and bombings and less and less on actual battles with South Vietnamese troops. The North Vietnamese decided that their friends in the south needed help. In December 1960, North Vietnamese soldiers began to hike south along the Ho Chi Minh Trail to assist the Viet Cong.

## THE FIGHTING GROWS

The number of United States military advisers quickly grew to twelve hundred—in a country most Americans could not find on a map. South Vietnamese soldiers and United States advisers went looking for the Viet Cong. If they went in large numbers, the Viet Cong hid. If they went in small numbers or camped out overnight, they were attacked and injured or killed. The South Vietnamese were supported by aircraft secretly flown by United States pilots. Because fighting by outsiders was against the 1954 agreement, for several years the United Stated denied being involved in any kind of combat.

Diem's problems grew. A division (ten thousand soldiers) of the Army of the Republic of Vietnam, or ARVN, was defeated by a small number of Viet Cong in the Mekong Delta. In Saigon, anti-Diem forces were annoyed by the obvious corruption. Buddhists protested all over South Vietnam and made world headlines in Saigon. There, on a June morning in 1963, a Buddhist monk poured gasoline on himself and set the fuel afire. He died in flames, seated at a major intersection. The suicide drew attention to mistreatment of Buddhists, but Diem forces continued to put Buddhists and others in airless, dirty prison cells.

ıown he was hated. How many heads of
r palaces bombed by planes from their own
)63, Diem's soldiers attacked and arrested
d Buddhist monks and nuns in Saigon's
... temple. Striking at night, the Diem police arrested
_ugious leaders all across the country. Martial law was imposed
in and around Saigon.

## THE END OF DIEM

American advisers realized that the Diem government was in
no position to stop the Communists. So when a group of South
Vietnamese generals hinted that they planned to overthrow Diem,
Americans said they would look the other way. On November 1,
1963, rebel generals placed troops all around Saigon and encircled
Diem's palace. Diem and his brother, Nhu, hid in the cellar. They
sneaked out a side door and later surrendered at a Catholic
church. Both were shot to death the next day and Saigon residents
celebrated.

The generals could neither run the country nor beat the enemy.
ARVN soldiers were losing more weapons than they captured.
They also were suffering more casualties than the Viet Cong. In
August 1964, the United States found a way to enter the war.
America claimed that a United States navy ship had been attacked
in international waters east of North Vietnam. President Lyndon
Johnson, who had become president in November 1963, following
the assassination of President John F. Kennedy, and Congress sent
military forces to Vietnam. The United States joined the South
Vietnamese, who were fighting for control of their country against
the Viet Cong guerrillas and the North Vietnamese.

# Chapter 5

# *TEN YEARS OF WAR*

North Vietnamese troops began to show up in larger numbers in South Vietnam in 1964. At the same time, the Viet Cong bombed offices, barracks, nightclubs, and restaurants. United States marines splashed ashore at Da Nang in central Vietnam in the spring of 1965. The war was escalating. The first big confrontation between North Vietnamese and American soldiers took place later in 1965 in a misty, jungle-clad area called the Ia Drang valley, near the border with Laos. Weeks of bitter fighting with rifles, machine guns, artillery, and air strikes resulted in the deaths of an estimated two thousand Communists. About three hundred Americans were reported killed.

Despite United States successes, the Communists took control of more and more central highlands territory. To stop the flow of weapons from the north, the United States sent jet fighter-bombers into North Vietnam. But bombing only seemed to make the North Vietnamese more determined. Peasant boys left their villages, underwent military training, and then began the long walk south, down the Ho Chi Minh Trail.

Unlike the well-armed North Vietnamese, the Viet Cong were not always given modern weapons. So the Viet Cong made booby traps out of artillery shells stolen from the Americans. They were

*One of the tunnels in Cu Chi*

buried and wired to go off when a truck or tank ran over them.
Hand grenades with wires rigged across a jungle trail could kill or
injure anyone who set them off. Holes in the ground, called *punji*
pits, were filled with bamboo spikes. Soldiers who stepped in
them suffered injuries that could lead to the loss of a leg. What the
Viet Cong lacked in weapons, they made up for in ingenuity. And
they kept getting better arms as the war progressed.

Still, they were no match with South Vietnamese or United
States forces in a firefight. If it appeared that the Viet Cong might
win a fight, the South Vietnamese or American troops could
always call in artillery or air strikes. To save themselves, the Viet
Cong dug elaborate tunnels, some several stories deep. They hid
in these carefully constructed places as bombs or shells were
dropped from above. Some tunnels had hospitals, warehouses,
and places for dozens of soldiers to rest. A complex near the city
of Cu Chi was built beneath a large United States army base. That
may have been the safest place in all of Vietnam for a Viet Cong to
hide.

Meanwhile, in the north, things were not going that smoothly. The Soviet Union and China, the two major suppliers of arms to North Vietnam, were hardly speaking to each other. Weapons put on trains in the Soviet Union for shipment across China to Vietnam were sometimes delayed. Ships from the two huge Communist countries sat for long periods before being unloaded. Although the ships themselves weren't bombed, everyone in the port of Haiphong hid as bombs rained on warehouses and military targets.

## KY TAKES CHARGE

In Saigon, Nguyen Cao Ky had taken charge of the government. Ky was Vietnam's most famous warrior, a handsome and skilled air force pilot who was born in the north but moved south to fight the Communists. He had the backing of most South Vietnamese military men when he came to power in 1965. But he did little to stamp out corruption, which was everywhere. Also, he failed to offer the people any reasons why they should not join the Viet Cong and the North Vietnamese. But for two years, the skillful Ky was able to convince the United States and other free-world countries that he might be the savior of South Vietnam.

Ky and the Americans herded large numbers of rural people into cities as part of a plan to create safe areas while denying the Viet Cong new members. But this plan was not well thought out. Families arrived in Saigon and other cities and had to live in cardboard boxes, sewer pipes, or in shacks. Families broke up and the number of orphans grew. This would have been sad in any society. But in Vietnam, with its close family ties and traditions centered around the same piece of land, it was tragic.

*Prime Minister (later vice-president) Nguyen Cao Ky (left) and President Nguyen Van Thieu (right)*

## REFORM FAILS

Prime Minister Ky was under pressure from the United States to end corruption. The United States wanted a democracy, not a military dictatorship. Back came the Buddhist street protesters, creating especially bitter dissent in the city of Da Nang. Ky attacked Da Nang with troops and planes. Not even public suicides by Buddhist monks and nuns prevented jailing of hundreds of protesters. Ky did schedule a national election, to be held in September 1967. More than 80 percent of the adults in South Vietnam went to the polls—and for good reason. Anyone caught after the election with no punch on his identity card could be accused of being a Communist. Ky ended up the vice-president, with General Nguyen Van Thieu elected president. The two received only 35 percent of the vote. An unknown attorney finished second with 17 percent.

# ROLLING THUNDER

Rolling Thunder was the bombing operation conducted by American fighter-bombers from 1965 to 1968. A million tons of missiles, bombs, and rockets fell on North Vietnam and on the Ho Chi Minh Trail. To hide from the planes, North Vietnamese soldiers in Laos dug caves where several trucks could be parked, some distance from the trail. Trucks moved by night without lights. Parts of the trail eventually were paved. But other parts were so tough to travel that a man pushing a bicycle could not go up and down the hills. The bombing slowed but failed to stop the flow of men and supplies.

Bombardment from the air was terrifying. B-52 bombers covered areas with bombs just as one might lay a carpet. Enemy troops huddled in fear as the bombs moved toward them, making shattering noises and hurling earth and trees and jagged bits of metal. After a bombing, wounded men staggered around, in shock. Blood ran from their noses, mouths, and ears. Sometimes, they were buried alive or burned with napalm, jellied gasoline that splashes along the ground like a wave across a beach. Or, they were wounded by phosphorus, which burned when exposed to air. Mere survival under such circumstances is unbelievable. The enemy also was bombarded with offers of money or land if they would give themselves up. This *chieu hoi*, or "open arms," program was a failure.

# THE TET OFFENSIVE

By the end of 1967, the United States had about 500,000 soldiers on duty in South Vietnam. The Communists were aware that the

*Da Lat burning after a bombing attack to dislodge the Viet Cong during the Tet Offensive*

war was not popular in America. That may have been one reason why they decided to attack all major United States and South Vietnamese positions during the annual lunar new year holiday known as Tet. The attacks took place all across Vietnam on January 29, 1968. Sappers—Viet Cong experts in explosives and commando-type operations—got onto many bases.

The worst loss of life took place at first in and around Saigon. Rockets and mortars were fired into neighborhoods and Viet Cong units took over large parts of the city. The Viet Cong failed to capture the government radio station, but they set up headquarters at a race track and held onto their positions for several days. Elsewhere in the country, provincial capitals were up for grabs as the Viet Cong and some North Vietnamese units caused huge losses in manpower, weapons, and supplies. The longest battle, and the heaviest loss of life among civilians, took place in Hue.

For centuries, the best minds in the country had gone to Hue to be educated. Modern graduates of Hue schools often ignored both

*After the war, the Royal Palace
at Hue was not destroyed (left),
but some parts of it, such as this column (above)
were badly riddled by bullets.*

the South Vietnamese government and the Communists. They
tried to follow an independent path, which caused resentment in
the north and south. Once Viet Cong and North Vietnamese units
took control of Hue in 1968, they executed hundreds of innocent,
free-thinking people.

Terrible fighting raged for almost a month in city streets, alleys,
sewers, and in the beautiful old temples and shrines that had
made Hue Vietnam's most romantic city. United States marines
and their Vietnamese counterparts paid with their lives for every
yard they advanced. Perhaps the battle would have ended quicker
if Americans had used air power and artillery. But they were
reluctant to destroy the fortlike citadel in Hue, a symbol to the
Vietnamese of their long and rich history.

## TET'S AFTERMATH

The Viet Cong had gone into the Tet battle convinced that there
would be a popular uprising. They expected people from all walks

of life to join them in overthrowing the Thieu government. It did not happen. Instead, the Viet Cong suffered terrible losses. They were virtually wiped out as a fighting force for several months. In the end, however, the South Vietnamese were the big losers. They lost the determination of the United States. Back home, Americans who watched the unceasing violence on the daily television news became unhappy with the war. The Tet Offensive of 1968 was the true turning point of the entire conflict.

A year later, there was a terrible incident that caused Americans to oppose the war more than ever. A unit of United States soldiers killed more than one hundred innocent women, children, and old people in a tiny village in northern South Vietnam called My Lai. It appears that most soldiers were convinced by their officers that all residents of the village were Viet Cong. Many were marched to a ditch and shot with automatic weapons. Because the Thieu government did not want the massacre known, it was censored when the story appeared a year later. But the killings frightened Vietnamese who learned of it. Who could they trust?

Peace negotiations began in 1968. But the United States did not pull out its last troops until 1973. By the time they left, America had spent $141 billion on military and economic aid. More important, almost fifty-eight thousand Americans had died.

The cease-fire negotiated in Paris displeased the South Vietnamese. They were said to be in control of their country but, in reality, northern troops were all over South Vietnam. President Nguyen Van Thieu did not want a cease-fire, and he ordered his soldiers to take as much territory as they could in the final days. The north did the same thing, storing weapons and supplies in the central highlands. The country remained unsafe and was about to become more so.

*Monks protesting government decrees that abolished many traditional Buddhist rights*

## AIR POWER

The north had agreed to the cease-fire in part because the
United States renewed bombing North Vietnam with ferocity in
late 1972. The north was attacked so often that the country ran
out of surface-to-air missiles, used to shoot down planes. Air
power in the south was less potent—United States forces took
many planes with them when they left. South Vietnam still had a
strong air force, but fuel and ammunition were no longer plentiful
and less maintenance was done on the aircraft.

Instead of trying to rally different leaders throughout the south,
Thieu jailed the ones he disliked. He censored or shut down
newspapers that dared to disagree with him. This time, Roman
Catholics joined Buddhists to protest the government's harsh
actions. Hanoi was cautious, in part because the Soviet Union and
China had reduced the flow of weapons and supplies when the
United States departed. Fighting in 1974 was subdued, but it
proved to be the lull before the storm.

# THE FALL OF THE SOUTH

The Communists had always attacked during the dry season, and 1975 was no exception. There were huge attacks in the central highlands. South Vietnamese soldiers retreated east, toward the coast—any way they could. Since their families often followed them around the country, women and children were caught in the retreat. Soldiers and families alike died as the Communists chased the retreating army, hammering the thirsty and hungry people with murderous artillery fire. The central highlands had fallen.

In Hue and Da Nang, residents saw the stragglers and that set off panic. People scrambled to get on boats, barges, or rafts. Soldiers panicked, trampling women and children in their effort to board boats. Bodies bobbed about the piers of Vietnam's coastal cities. There was mayhem on the boats, as people died from exertion or from lack of water. By the thousands, they vacated central Vietnam. The Communists entered Da Nang and told everyone to go about their business. Enemy soldiers continued south.

ARVN members made a last stand at a town called Xuan Loc, sixty miles (ninety-seven kilometers) north of Saigon. The South Vietnamese fought bravely but were eventually outnumbered and pushed back toward their capital. United States advisers told President Thieu he might be wise to leave. He did so on April 25, 1975, taking millions of dollars worth of gold. The Communists were so close to Saigon they could hit it with rockets or artillery. Many pro-American Vietnamese were left behind in the rush to board helicopters that ferried people to United States ships waiting offshore. On the afternoon of April 30, 1975, North Vietnamese forces rolled into Saigon. The war was over. It had cost the lives of 1.3 million Vietnamese.

# Chapter 6

# POSTWAR HARDSHIPS

The North Vietnamese troops who entered Saigon amazed the South Vietnamese. They were either young or old. Troops between the ages of twenty and forty had been killed in the years of fighting. The youngsters were ignorant of the war and its impact on Vietnam and on world affairs. These were farm boys, young men who put down their hoes and shovels and went through brief training before being sent south. They were directed by a small number of veterans from as early as the war with the French in the 1950s.

The Communists emptied the jails, believing that anyone jailed by the old government must be pro-Communist. They then began to refill the cells, primarily with mid-level officials of the Thieu government. High-level officials were often executed, though this fact was not known for several years. Others were assigned to thirty days in reeducation camps, which were set up to convince the South Vietnamese that the new Communist way of doing things was best. The camps were crude and people sent to them were sometimes shot if they tried to leave. To this day, there may be Buddhists, Catholics, and various officials held in camps against their will.

## STARVATION LOOMS

The North Vietnamese wanted to ease the south into the
Communist system. In doing this, they were hampered by poor
agricultural production, corruption, some continued fighting in
the south, and a black-market economy that was more trusted
than the old or new government. Honest people were going
hungry. Even some persons involved in the black market were
unable to find food, even though they had money. To end black-
market sales, the government changed the currency overnight.
People who went to bed with money, woke up with worthless
pieces of paper. Most of the free enterprise dealers and black
marketeers fled the country.

Those who wanted to leave were charged huge sums (as much
as $2 thousand per person) by the government. All they got for
their money was the chance to board an unsafe boat and risk
death on the high seas. Thai and Malay pirates routinely robbed
these boat people, as they were called. They also died from lack of
water or from starvation. From 1978 through 1982, thousands left.
Many hundreds died in trying to find another land that would let
them become citizens. Only recently, due to United Nations and
other pressure, has the Vietnamese government stopped this cruel
way to get rid of its anti-Communists.

Because Vietnamese and Cambodian people have sometimes
failed to live in peace, their border often has been dangerous.
Cambodian forces, under the leadership of Pol Pot, crossed the
border in 1975 to kill Vietnamese civilians. The Vietnamese
decided to punish Pol Pot, who also approved killing many of his
own people. Vietnamese soldiers marched in Cambodia and
chased the *Khmer Rouge* (Red Cambodians) west into remote hills

near Thailand. Since China was an ally of Pol Pot, this caused the Vietnam-China relationship to decline even more.

## VIETNAM VERSUS CHINA

After warning the Vietnamese to leave Cambodia for several years, the Chinese attacked Vietnam. All along the northern border, fighting flared. As many as eighty thousand Chinese troops fought their way through heavy artillery and across mountain passes into the land of their new enemy. Fighting was bitter and the Vietnamese finally were able to stop the Chinese after losing the provincial capital of Lang Son. Chinese forces retreated slowly a couple of weeks later, destroying civilian and military property as they departed. To this day, the Chinese-Vietnamese border is heavily patrolled. The brief war made the Soviet Union and Vietnam firmer allies than ever.

## DISCRIMINATION

Everyone was doing without in postwar Vietnam, but one small minority was having a harder time than others. These young people were the sons and daughters of American military men and Vietnamese women. Some were able to live with their mothers, who had not left the country. But others had been unplanned births and were not welcome. These children found themselves on the street. They lived by begging or by doing jobs no one else wanted. All were in what used to be South Vietnam. There were as many as twelve thousand such orphans.

The government was in no hurry to help these children, even though some of their fathers and other United States citizens were

*Above: Amerasian children*
*Right: A boy carries his father, a disabled veteran.*

concerned for their welfare. Vietnamese leaders had been promised an estimated $3.5 billion by former United States President Nixon. They wanted this money to rebuild their factories and to begin new public works projects. But Nixon resigned from office and the dollars were never sent to Vietnam. So one of the ways the Vietnamese annoyed Americans was to give them little or no information about the Amerasian children, as they came to be called.

Unlike most stories, the lives of the Amerasians has a somewhat happy ending. In 1987, the Vietnamese said they would begin allowing Amerasian children to leave the country. An orderly departure program, which also has decreased the number of boat people, is now under way. The United States has made some concessions, too. America has asked humanitarian groups to donate medicine, medical care, artificial limbs, and rehabilitation to the Vietnamese. These small acts may help restore diplomatic relations between the two nations. If that is the case, the nagging problem of the United States prisoners of war not yet accounted for may be answered.

# MISSING PRISONERS OF WAR

The North Vietnamese let American prisoners of war (POWs) go after the United States left Vietnam in 1973. But did they let all prisoners go, or were some kept against their will in prison or labor camps? The Vietnamese have insisted that there are no living Americans being held against their will anywhere in Vietnam. Approximately twenty-five hundred were missing at the end of the war and many of them were pilots or air crews whose planes went down over the north. If they parachuted, then they should be alive, the United States reasoned.

Other factors entered in. Enemies of the Communists told United States authorities that they had seen Americans in labor camps in the north. But were these sightings real or were they made up so that the tribe member might be given a new life in the United States? Some fifteen years have passed since the last American soldier departed Vietnam. If there are any prisoners left, they are a well-kept secret.

The new general secretary of the Vietnamese Communist party, Nguyen Van Linh, told a reporter in the fall of 1987 that there were no American POWs anywhere in the country. One way to prove that of course would be to renew diplomatic relations between the two countries. Then, United States citizens could go to Vietnam and have a look for themselves. The best guess is that there are no living prisoners left.

# CHANGING LEADERSHIP

After more than ten years of trying to pull the country together, Vietnam's three top leaders resigned. This resignation took place

*Pham Van Dong*    *Le Duc Tho*    *Truong Chinh*

late in 1986 and included Communist party Secretary General
Truong Chinh, Prime Minister Pham Van Dong, and key
Politburo member Le Duc Tho. These resignations shocked the
world—it was as if the president, vice-president, and secretary of
state of the United States had suddenly quit. The three Vietnamese
were aging, but they had become famous for guiding the north to
victory in the war. All three were close to Ho Chi Minh and they
helped lead North Vietnam following Ho's death in 1969. At one
time or another, they had fought French, Japanese, Americans,
Cambodians, and Chinese. That was the problem: the men could
wage war, but were unable to improve the country once peace
arrived. Two months later, a dozen top ministers were fired.

## FORM OF GOVERNMENT

Vietnam has never enjoyed a democratic form of government.
The Vietnamese always have been led by people who told them
what was best for them. The people never have been able to tell
their government what they think is best. That was true before

Europeans arrived, when the Chinese, a series of kings, or the occasional gang of bandits ran all or parts of the country. It continued to be so once the French took control. And it was true when the country was split into North and South Vietnam.

Today's government was formed on April 25, 1976. On that day, Vietnamese voted to elect members to a National Assembly. This body has 492 seats and it is divided almost equally between members from the north and members from the south. The members were elected by eligible voters—all persons over the age of eighteen. The assembly's first job was to unite the divided land. On July 2, 1976, the assembly elected a president, two vice-presidents, a cabinet, and other political and governmental offices and committees.

One committee began to work on a constitution, which was finished in 1979. It was to be enforced in stages, but because of the fighting in Cambodia and the border war with China, the country fell back on a set of laws created for the north in 1960. This document claimed that people had many rights, but pointed out that these rights were under the control of the Vietnamese Communist party and the state. It said that no one could use any of his or her freedoms to attack the state. Provisions were made for minorities, but these hill-dwelling people (and the Chinese) lost all self-government shortly after the war ended.

The National Assembly works with the council of ministers, whom they pick. These ministers oversee departments, such as defense and health and education. Until 1986, the government was a bureaucracy. The shake-up that occurred in late 1986 and early 1987 has reduced the great number of bureaucrats. This has forced some people to find meaningful work. They are no longer dependent on the government for a job.

*Nguyen Van Linh (left) and the sixth Vietnamese Communist Party Congress in 1986*

On a regional level, there are thirty-five provinces and three municipalities (Hanoi, Haiphong, and Ho Chi Minh City). Each is run by a people's council. There also is a local people's council to run districts. These areas of the country each contain about 100,000 people. And each village is operated by a local people's council.

## ONE-PARTY RULE

There is only one political party and it has been around since Ho Chi Minh formed it in 1930. That is the Vietnamese Communist party. About 1.5 million people, or 2.5 percent of the population, belong. It is open to anyone of eighteen years or older. The party is controlled by a committee called the Politburo. There are fourteen members and three alternates. There is also a central committee, beneath the Politburo, with 101 full members and 32 alternates. The general secretary of the Politburo, Nguyen Van Linh, is an economist and a reformer who prodded the older members to retire in 1986.

*A Vietnamese commando (left) and soldiers on patrol (right)*

Communist countries are highly organized, and Vietnam is no exception. Every youth group, farmers' organization, women's club, or religious congregation is overseen by the party and has members who report to the party. During the war, there were other political organizations, but they worked with the Communists and against the south. These included the National Liberation Front of South Vietnam, also known as the Viet Cong. There are no active anti-Communist organizations today.

When Saigon fell, and for a while afterward, it was impossible to separate the justice system from the military. That is because soldiers were used to enforce the law and to dispense justice. Thieves who were caught, tried, and convicted sometimes found themselves in front of military firing squads. Fortunately for everyone, a more conventional system of courts is in operation in the country today.

## A MIGHTY MILITARY

There are about 1,100,000 men in Vietnam's armed forces. As many as 140,000 Vietnamese soldiers are in Cambodia. The very best troops are now guarding the border with China. After the war, the military was used as a place where men could be "stored" until there were jobs for them. Many men had no skills and had known nothing but how to fight. Total active-duty personnel now is about 500,000, but there are twice that many reserves.

## IMPORTS AND EXPORTS

Modern Vietnam has many needs, but little money. It exports inexpensive rice, raw rubber, wood, and fruits and vegetables. Coal and various minerals are beginning to be mined and shipped overseas, too. Most goods go to either the Soviet Union or Japan. Petroleum products, steel and other metals, railroad equipment, and chemicals and medicine are imported in quantity from the Soviets and the Japanese. The Soviets have propped up the government with millions of dollars in aid.

Because the economy has been so dismal, the government has looked the other way as hundreds of acres of opium poppies are grown. Some experts believe the government actually supports growing opium so that it can get money for the empty treasury. Vietnam has been involved in the opium trade since the French introduced it more than a century ago.

The only successful part of the economy is the black market. People in most cities illegally exchange Vietnamese money for foreign currency. Or, they may trade a pig for a bag of rice, or a bottle of wine for flashlight batteries. Black markets turn up wherever the economy fails to meet people's needs. It is subdued in the north, where people live simple lives. But business is brisk in southern cities, where the desire for consumer goods is as strong as ever.

Thatch-roofed houses in a typical rural village (above) and vegetable gardens flourishing on the edge of the city of Da Lat (below)

# Chapter 7

# LIFE IN VIETNAM

---

## VILLAGE LIFE

Vietnam's big cities used to make headlines, but the heart of the country is its thousands of tiny, rural villages. Life has not changed much for hundreds of years in rural Vietnam. That is both good and bad news. The good news is that this lack of change gives Vietnamese a wonderful sense of who they are and where they live. It teaches them to respect the land and its people. But there is plenty of bad news in rural areas.

For centuries, small farmers and landless peasants were at the mercy of everything and everyone. The weather could and did ruin crops on a regular basis. If a rice crop withered, the farmer had to turn to someone with money. That person charged the farmer very high interest rates. These rates kept the farmer and his family forever in debt. Taxes were demanded, too. They drove rural families deeper in debt. Landlords could increase the price of rented farmland at a moment's notice. And the climate made it hard to stay healthy.

*Because of underdevelopment, farming methods are antiquated. Above: A rice farmer stands on his wooden plow and guides his water buffalo team across a rice paddy. Right: Another farmer uses a foot-operated waterwheel for irrigation.*

Farmers today still lead difficult lives. They arise early and eat a small breakfast of rice or fruit before heading for the rice paddy. There they plow, open and shut paddy dikes for irrigation, plant, transplant, or harvest. As noontime temperatures pass 90 degrees Fahrenheit (32.2 degrees Celsius), the farmer returns to his home. The family eats its largest meal of the day. After the meal, the farmer may smoke his pipe while his wife chews a tangy betel nut. They drink several cups of tea, then take naps.

This routine keeps the family out of the broiling sun (or monsoon rain) for two hours each day. The farmer returns to the paddy in midafternoon, working until evening. He has a meal, then may meet neighbors to discuss farming or other subjects. Almost all farmers are men. But women play a great role in the economic welfare of the family.

*A woman harvesting rice*

Besides assisting the husband, women keep the home and see to it that each family member has at least one outfit in good repair. Rural men and women usually wear baggy, pajamalike garments that are easily rolled up when it becomes necessary to wade in the paddy mud. Pointed, conical straw hats keep off the sun and rain. Children wear T-shirts and shorts and go barefoot.

Virtually every Vietnamese home has an altar in a prominent place. This altar is covered with red and gold paper, and holds smoldering incense, candles, scrolls, and snacks for offerings. Whether the family is Buddhist or Christian, it is likely that members are aware of, and worship, several generations of their ancestors.

Rice, the mainstay of Vietnam, is its
most important crop. Top: A bamboo scarecrow is
used in a highlands rice field.
Right: Rice paper is made in an orphanage.
Above: Man working in rice paddy

# RICE-PLANTING RITUALS

Rice shoots must be carefully transplanted by hand when the seedlings are about one month old. Transplanting is an important time, as farmers and their families gather in the paddies. Each tiny rice plant is carefully planted in a few inches of muddy water. Later on, wives and children will help weed and fertilize. All family members work seven days a week.

Great improvements have been made in rice technology. Modern rice grows quickly. There can be harvests twice a year in tropical areas such as the Mekong Delta. The rice grows to be almost waist high before bending with the weight of the kernels. When the plants are mature, the paddies are drained. The plants are cut and threshed. Threshing knocks the rice off the grasslike plant. Little is wasted: the plant is used for animal feed, for brewing, for making grass mats, and for fertilizer. Rice also is the country's leading export.

Vietnam is one of the top five rice-producing countries on earth—and that includes the much larger countries of India and China. Immediately after the war between North and South Vietnam, the peasants of the newly unified country prevented outright starvation by producing rice crops.

Vietnam was able to export rice for the first time since the end of the war in 1985. But a poor harvest year followed immediately: they imported 100,000 tons (over 90,000,000 kilograms) of rice from Indonesia late in 1986. Payment was a promise to repay the rice with 120,000 tons (over 109,000,000 kilograms) of rice at a later date. The country had no currency to spare, even for food.

There are three different kinds of rice growing in the country. Mekong Delta farmers grow their rice in paddies, where earthen

*Cleaning the day's catch of fish*

dikes are used to manage the water level. Northern residents more often grow their crop in dry fields. Mountain tribes grow a unique type of hill rice that, when cooked, is as sticky as the frosting on a cake.

## HOMEGROWN FOOD

While rice is served at almost every meal, there are many other important foods. Fish is a steady source of protein and is hauled in by hundreds of people in small, oceangoing boats each day. The fish is often dried, since there is little refrigeration. Or, it ends up in the rice bowl as *nuoc mam*, a fermented sauce that has a strong odor but a mild taste. Freshwater fish is netted or trapped in nearby rivers and canals or raised in small farm ponds. Eggs, frogs, and eels are other sources of protein.

*A variety of fruits (left), and ducks and chickens for sale (right), are common sights in city markets.*

Meat is not a common sight on the ends of chopsticks. It is just too expensive. Farmers raise chickens, geese, and perhaps a pig or a water buffalo, but large animals are eaten only on special occasions. Pork or beef are seen only at festivals or weddings or other infrequent events. A member of the hill-dwelling Hmong tribe, now living in the United States, pointed out that one chicken served his large family for almost a week in their former home in Vietnam.

Vegetables are an important part of the diet and are grown in small plots near the home. Onions, manioc, young bamboo shoots, sugarcane, soybeans, yams, and other root crops are served regularly. So is fruit. Bananas, mangos, mangosteens, and coconuts are grown in trees that have been planted very close to the home and offer the usually modest Vietnamese some shade and privacy.

*Left: Getting a ride to work*
*Right: Removing cement block from its mold and setting it out to dry*

Since the war ended in 1975, thousands of refugees who sought safety in big cities have returned to the countryside. One of the problems of the new government was to find these people meaningful work. Many thought of themselves as rural residents, but they had grown up living any way they could in the big cities. State farms were begun to employ these people, who had little or no farming experience. Whether state farming can be as productive as individual farming remains to be seen. It is the intention of the government to get rid of large landlords.

## A CITY FAMILY

Life in one of Vietnam's major cities or provincial capitals is no easier than life in the country. A typical husband may be employed as a construction worker, digging ditches, carrying

*Street vendors sell an assortment of tasty dishes.*

concrete blocks, or constructing frames for buildings. He is paid by the government and his annual wage may be only about 1,800 dong ($200) a year. His day begins with a quick and early breakfast of *pho*, a hot soup made of noodles and onions with bits of beef in it. This nourishing meal originated in the northern part of the country and is now a breakfast favorite in many cities. Hot tea accompanies most meals.

Pho is just one of the many foods sold by street vendors. The Vietnamese are great snackers and buy things to sip and nibble with their meager pay. Tiny meatballs, no bigger than marbles, are cooked over a charcoal fire built in any empty artillery shell. Other vendors sell noodles in a variety of tasty sauces, rice cakes, warm eggs, candy, and more. The many tidbits combine ideas from two of the world's great schools of cooking, the French and the Chinese. Soft drinks, tea, beer, and rice wine wash it all down.

*A glimpse at the interior of an apartment (left) and a home (right) in Ho Chi Minh City*

Like the farmer, the city worker eats his largest meal and then relaxes when the heat of the day is most intense. He works into the evening before returning to his home, which may be one end of an old military barracks, a tiny apartment in an old building, or new, low-cost, wood-and-mat government houses. The home will no doubt have a central area for ancestor worship, the same as a rural dwelling.

The city wife has probably worked all day, too. She may have welded, prepared food in a cannery, or served as a helper in a clinic where babies are born. If her home is quite small or if she cooks over wood or charcoal, she may make much of her meals outdoors. She will have purchased food for each meal on her way home from work, since refrigeration is scarce. Women make up almost two-thirds of the work force and they are highly productive. But they are not treated as equals yet in this part of the world.

*A Montagnard village (left) and some of its inhabitants (right)*

## THE MONTAGNARDS

Besides lowland villagers and city residents, there is a third part of the population. The central highlands are peopled with tribes who were all termed *Montagnards,* or mountain dwellers, by the French. They look different and speak a different language than the other Vietnamese. Hill dwellers are most easily identified by their colorful clothing and jewelry. Some tribes are tattooed and others file their front teeth. They tend not to live in the same place for long, but move where their special kind of farming takes them.

Without plows or other modern implements, the hill tribes practice slash-and-burn agriculture. They make deep cuts into all the trees in a small area of jungle. These cuts cause the sap to dry up and the trees die. Then, tribespeople set the area on fire. The trees burn quickly. The ashes that are left enrich the poor hilltop soil enough so that sticky rice, root crops, and cash crops can be grown.

*Montagnard hunters*

Like the lowland farmer, Montagnards grow, trap, catch, or shoot everything they need except tea, salt, cloth, and items such as toys. One way to get money for these goods is to grow opium poppies. Opium has been sold by the tribes for more than a century. It is obtained by making a razor-thin cut in the pod of the unripe poppy flower. The sticky, white juice that oozes out can be processed to make legal medicine such as morphine or illegal drugs such as heroin. Much of the world's heroin comes from tribespeople in Vietnam and elsewhere in Southeast Asia.

Some hill people were trained by American Green Beret soldiers to fight the Communists during the Vietnam War. Because of this, the new government has mistreated the Meos and other tribes. Those who have tried to escape to Thailand by traveling west through Laos and across the upper Mekong River have sometimes been killed by Vietnamese soldiers in Laos.

*Schoolchildren in Ho Chi Minh City*

## EDUCATION

It has been said that families who follow Confucianism produce children who want to learn. That is because this philosophy values education and because school in Vietnam has always held the promise of a better life.

Assuming a Vietnamese child lives in an area that has returned to more or less normal after the war, he or she will begin school at the age of five. Elementary school lasts five years. School runs for four hours a day, six days a week, all year long. Students are taught morality and government, history, geography, mathematics, drawing, physical education, home economics, and home care. At the age of ten, a student receives a certificate showing that he or she has completed elementary school.

Secondary school is four years long and includes all of the subjects listed above, plus a foreign language, world literature, and crafts. An examination is given at the end of four years. Based on the results of the examination, students can then go to vocational-technical school, high school, or directly to work. High school has all of the subjects mentioned and is three years long. An examination is held and those who pass it are given a diploma. Diplomas mean high paying jobs and increased respect.

Since 1975, an increasing number of students who do well in high school or vocational school are sent out of the country to study. They most often go to the Soviet Union or to an Eastern European country in the Communist bloc. Some critics of the present government believe these work-study students are little better than slaves, being sent to the Soviet Union to work long hours for little money so that Vietnam can pay back its enormous debt to the Soviet Union. Nothing has been proven. However, it is no doubt more enjoyable for a person with a good technical mind to end up in the polytechnic college that has successfully produced engineers for several decades in Hanoi.

## THE POPULATION PROBLEM

Rural and city couples alike usually are young and have several children. Rapid population growth is one of the country's most pressing problems. With health care improving and with many people of childbearing age, Vietnam simply does not know where to put everyone. In fact, one of the reasons the army is so large (over one million men) is that there is little work and nowhere for these soldiers to live. Like many people in underdeveloped countries, the Vietnamese have always valued large families. Getting the population under control is a major task. A step toward this goal is being taken by the government. It rewards persons who control family size.

City and country dwellers have other problems. There remain

*Left: A family in front of their home*
*Right: A young boy crippled by shrapnel injuries from a leftover bomb*

in many parts of the country unexploded bombs, shells, and other potentially deadly leftovers of the war. Hardly a day goes by when a farmer or manual laborer causes an explosion with his or her plow or shovel. There are already thousands of amputees and other disabled persons from the war; many are without artificial limbs, in constant pain, and have little hope.

Tropical diseases also are a problem. Malaria is widespread, in part because most Vietnamese do not have easy access to the pills that prevent it. Tuberculosis is common among people by the time they reach adulthood. Other medical problems include rabies, typhoid, dysentery, and parasitic and childhood diseases.

Lead content in rivers and canals around Ho Chi Minh City is far above safe levels. Standing water contains huge amounts of human and animal waste and is not safe to be near. Foods show

*Herbicides, used during the Vietnam War, destroyed vegetation that will take many years to grow back.*

varying amounts of pesticides, herbicides, fertilizers, and substances that have gotten into the food chain as a result of the war.

One of the most evident problems is the aftereffects of Agent Orange. Agent Orange was an herbicide (plant killer) used by United States forces. The herbicide was sprayed on thick jungles to deny the enemy a place to hide. The substance also killed food crops and rubber trees and may have caused cancer and serious birth defects among children of Vietnamese and American veterans. Between 1965 and 1971, about 8.6 million acres (over 3.4 million hectares) were sprayed with Agent Orange. The countryside today shows bare areas that may not grow anything for one hundred years, scientists estimate.

## TODAY'S TYPICAL VIETNAMESE

It's always risky to make sweeping statements about people in a country. But in general, the Vietnamese in any given village try to

*Young people in Vietnam today*

cooperate and avoid argument or competition. Whereas westerners are quick to turn to lawyers when arguments arise, the Vietnamese believe only persons of low intelligence need to go to a third party to settle a disagreement. They think westerners lack deep feelings and are naive. And they are convinced that constant praise shows a lack of sincerity.

There is little touching, although one may see two young persons of the same sex holding hands in a big city. Everyone is modest and women are quite shy.

Who, then, is a typical Vietnamese? He or she is young, perhaps twenty-six or twenty-seven years of age, able to read, married, the parent of three children, under slight pressure from the government to stop having children, the owner of hardly any possessions, and one who earns only about $500 per year. His or her mate will work, too.

Neither has much time for sports or leisure. Free time, if there is any, may be spent scavenging piles of building materials or working on a public-works project such as road repair. Life is hard and holds little immediate promise for improvement.

*Worshipers light incense in a temple in Ho Chi Minh City.*

# *Chapter 8*

# *RELIGION AND*
# *PHILOSOPHY*

---

Most Vietnamese do not consider themselves religious. True, there are numerous Buddhist *bonzes* (religious officials) and Catholic priests. But less than half of the population belongs to any organized religion. Yet the Vietnamese way of life is deeply influenced by a philosophy that is close to being a religion.

## CONFUCIANISM

During the one thousand years of Chinese domination, the Vietnamese came to know the beliefs of Confucius well. He was a Chinese philosopher who was born about 550 B.C. He developed guidelines that told people how they should behave. High morals and ethics, honest government, and sound education were greatly valued. Rulers were expected to protect their citizens, who were to be treated as their own children. In return, citizens maintained order by honoring good rulers.

Confucianism was brought to Vietnam by the Chinese, who found that this philosophy kept people peaceful, so long as they thought they were being protected. Equally important, it created a class of government officals called *mandarins*. These men ran local, provincial, and national offices for the Chinese and, later, for the

French. Mandarins lost importance as the French took complete control of Vietnam. But the respect shown teachers and village officials is a sign that Confucianism is as important to the Vietnamese as any religion.

## TAOISM

Taoism began in China even earlier than Confucianism. It is a religion founded by a man named Lao-Tzu, who taught followers to believe in the occult (the spirit world). He thought man's relationship with the universe was very important. Other interesting things about the religion include ancestor worship, which takes place in almost all Vietnamese homes, and *geomancy*, the importance of how things line up with the earth. Where to build a house, where to dig a grave, the direction your front door faces—all of these things and more are of concern to Taoists and to Vietnamese. Few Vietnamese today practice this religion, but many have been influenced by it.

## BUDDHISM

There are more Buddhists in Vietnam than members of any other faith. They may total six million or more. Buddhism came to Southeast Asia from India. It teaches that people are born again and again and again, in human and animal forms. A good person, the Buddhists say, keeps being born into better lives and eventually reaches *nirvana*—nonexistence. Buddhism is a religion of personal examination and experience, so there are no formal services. Believers go to Buddhist shrines to get into the proper frame of mind for self-improvement by looking inward.

*Above: Offerings are left on a table inside a Buddhist temple.*
*Left: A Buddhist temple of the Cham people*

There are different kinds of Buddhism in Vietnam. Northerners believe only priests can reach nirvana, whereas southerners think all followers of Buddha can make it. There is also at least one major sect, called Hoa Hao. This version of Buddhism has more than a million followers in the Mekong Delta and was founded there earlier in the twentieth century.

The modern Vietnamese who is serious about Buddhism is an activist. He or she wants justice for all. This has made the government unsure of the loyalty of its Buddhists. This mistrust is also due to the fact that many members of the Chinese minority are practicing Buddhists. There may be some Buddhist leaders under arrest at present in Vietnam.

## CATHOLICISM

The French brought Roman Catholicism to Vietnam. There are as many as four million Vietnamese Catholics and most are opposed to communism. In fact, almost all members of the South

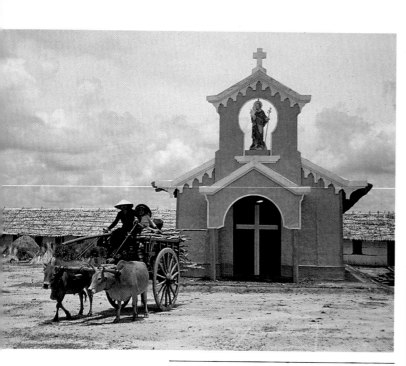

Above: A Catholic church in a rural area
Right: A religious leader performs
anamist rights at a funeral.

Vietnamese government were Catholics. Many of them fled south by boat after Vietnam was split in two by the 1954 peace treaty. More also tried to leave Vietnam after 1975.

Catholics have tended to be city dwellers. They were frequently well educated in French-language schools operated by priests or other Catholics.

During the war, several different Christian churches sent missionaries to Vietnam. Most directed the flow of church money, goods, and medicine to those most in need. Groups such as the Society of Friends (Quakers) provided hundreds of injured Vietnamese with artificial limbs and rehabilitation. The Mennonites worked to improve the lives of farmers. Other churches built schools. These American, Canadian, and Australian men and women have since been ordered to leave the country.

*The elaborate interior of a Cao Dai cathedral*

## ANIMISM

Dozens of primitive religions exist among tribes in the central highlands. Together, these forms of worship are called animism. Believers think that such things as storm clouds, forests, or rivers have souls. There are fewer believers today than earlier, because tribe members have either been neglected or forced to leave by the Vietnamese majority.

## CAO DAI

A religion founded in 1919 in the city of Tay Ninh has more than a million followers. With its own army, it is one of the most unusual movements of this century. Cao Dai is a mixture of many religions. Saints include Christ, Buddha, and other religious figures, plus great men and women down through history. For example, Joan of Arc is considered a Cao Dai saint. The figure of a Chinese dragon horse carrying a horoscope sits atop the main Cao Dai church. Like all religions today, the government fears activism by members and controls church activity.

## TET

Imagine a holiday where Christmas, July 4, and your birthday are all celebrated in one three-day party. That's how important the Tet (lunar new year) holiday is to the Vietnamese.

The festivities take place during the full moon prior to spring planting. That can be anytime from late January to mid-February. Vietnamese all over the country return to their parents' home, bringing food and gifts. Tet is when debts are repaid, mistakes corrected, forgiveness asked, and family and ancestors remembered. It is a mixture of happiness and noise, seriousness and quiet.

Tet is included in information about religion because it came out of ancient religious beliefs in China four thousand years ago. Much of the meaning has been lost, but we can guess that the first Tet observers wanted a good harvest. Today, Tet is a time to review the past, enjoy the present, and plan for the future.

There are many symbols associated with the holiday. One is the peach tree branch. Flowering branches are put in a vase in Vietnamese homes. Firecrackers light up the sky each night. Red and gold paper is seen everywhere as a decoration. Sacrifices of food are made to the new year.

Everyone celebrates the holiday, no matter what his or her

religious beliefs. That is why many military campaigns were begun at this time during the Vietnam War—there were few enemy soldiers on guard. The rest were at home with their families.

## GEOMANCY

Geomancy is a belief so old—and so unrelated to the modern world—that the word is hard to find in some dictionaries. Geomancy is transforming ordinary landscape into something important. For example, the direction a dead father's grave faces is said to affect the fortunes of his son. Is this sort of thing believed in? Well, when the Viet Cong wanted to do the worst thing they could in 1975 to former head of state Nguyen Van Thieu, they dug up and scattered the bones of his ancestors. His grief was heavy.

The late President Ngo Dinh Diem had his father's grave created in the shape of a turtle, a very lucky sign. To improve the burial site even more, he hired an architect to design and build a small, kidney-shaped pool near the grave. During construction of the pond, the neck of the sacred turtle was cut. Shortly afterward, Diem was overthrown and killed. Some Vietnamese believe the explanation for his fall lies in careless construction of the little pool.

The principles of geomancy are known to people called geomancers. They are consulted by Vietnamese Catholics or Buddhists or Communists before ground is broken for a building, before a tunnel is blasted through a hill, or before a site for a cemetery is chosen. Their skills involve reading good and bad winds, tapping the energy of the earth, and deciding how the stars are affecting the earth on any given day.

*Above: A craftsman with his colorful handmade masks*
*Left: Designs being hand sewn on silk cloth*

# Chapter 9

# *THE CULTURE OF*
# *VIETNAM*

---

For longer than most Vietnamese can remember, war ravaged
Vietnam. It overshadowed the fact that the country has been a
major contributor to the classic art and culture of Southeast Asia.

## POETRY

Even today, after generations of conflict, the people still
memorize classic Vietnamese poetry and write their own verses.
Poetry is much more common in Vietnam than in most other
countries. For example, a Vietnamese boy who is interested in a
girl will speak to her poetically. He may ask her if she is the only
flower in her garden. That is his way of asking if she has a
boyfriend. In turn, she could tell him that her garden awaits a
single strong plant.

Not all of the poetry is new or involves courtship. Vietnam's most famous epic poem is *Kim Van Kieu*, the story of a girl's struggle to maintain the honor of her family. The plot is long and involved, yet many Vietnamese have memorized the entire poem. *Kim Van Kieu* is such an accurate reflection of the Vietnamese soul that a prominent Vietnamese government official told Americans to quit relying on their statistics and pay more attention to this story.

A great deal of poetry, for and against warfare, was produced during the conflict. Buddhist monks, who are pacifists, swayed Vietnamese citizens with dramatic poems on the futility of war and the harm caused by foreign intruders. Another popular theme was nationalism: love of country. Many dead soldiers' belongings included poems they had written. The themes were familiar. Each poet tried to shrug off fear, fever, illness, or lack of sanitation so that the revolution could continue. Such sentiments showed the determination of the Viet Cong and North Vietnamese.

## LITERATURE

The Vietnamese language uses the Roman alphabet. It also has numerous accent marks that help the reader in pronunciation. Because of its melodic sound, poetry recited aloud has always been more popular than literature that is read silently. Yet there are epic stories in Vietnamese that, like most poems, are derived from the Chinese. The hopes and dreams of the nation are reflected in these epics, which tell of heroes and their efforts to save family and nation.

*A lacquer ware workshop in Ho Chi Minh City*

## ART

Lacquer ware is found throughout Vietnam. Wood is painted, then covered with coats of rich, clear, glossy liquid. The painting is protected from the tropical climate with shiny layers of cellulose that is dissolved in solvents. The cellulose can come from a tree or from tree sap.

Now that the war is over, block prints created in the tiny village of Dong Hoi for centuries are popular once again. Peasants there carve scenes on flat blocks of wood, cover the scenes with ink, and press the block onto paper. The scenes, such as children playing flutes while riding water buffalo, suggest the peace that has for so long eluded the Vietnamese. The scenes are unique and can be found for sale all over the country. They are common gifts during Tet celebrations.

*A colonial administration building in Hanoi, built by the French*

## ARCHITECTURE

Before the fighting that has torn the country, there were two great kinds of buildings. The French erected marvelous municipal and plantation offices and homes that looked as if they were picked up from somewhere in the French countryside and set down in Hue or Da Nang. The other style of building was Chinese, seen in the fortresslike citadel at Hue and in Buddhist temples. Less interesting, but seen everywhere, are the two-story shop houses. These narrow buildings contain a small store on the first floor and rooms for the merchant and his family on the second.

## MUSIC

Vietnamese music is poetry that is sung. It has a sad, almost eerie quality and has a different rhythm or cadence. In central Vietnam, orchestras using the five-tone Chinese scale still can be

heard. The instruments used include oboes, flutes, drums, and xylophone-type keyboards. Western rock and roll was played well by a few Vietnamese during the war, but the music is seldom heard today in the country.

## CLOTH AND CLOTHING

Except for the beautiful *ao dai* outfit (a blouse with flowing panels over long pants) worn by some Vietnamese women, the lowland Vietnamese have produced little unusual cloth or clothing. The various highland tribes, however, make wonderful costumes on their looms. Whether a member of the Black Tai,

*Left: A Montagnard woman wearing distinctive earrings*
*Right: Browsing at a book and magazine stand in Ho Chi Minh City*

White Tai, Hmong, Rhade, or other group, the costume is beautiful and different. Persons who have lived for a while in the highlands can tell which tribe a Montagnard is from by his or her clothing or jewelry. The cloth is made up of thousands of tiny, repeated patterns. Outfits take weeks to make. Many feature beads or pieces of silver attached to the costume. With silver hoops or other bits added, the wearer is sure to attract attention.

For the last one hundred years, French culture has greatly influenced the Vietnamese. Every person who received a high school diploma had been exposed to such French literary greats as Victor Hugo, Gustave Flaubert, Honoré de Balzac, and others. To this day, books written in French are available at street-corner stalls.

# Chapter 10

# FAMOUS VIETNAMESE

---

This small country may have been without a lot of things down through the years. But there has never been a shortage of people willing to fight for Vietnam. Whenever the family or the nation was threatened, men and women stepped forward in defense. The most famous patriot is Ho Chi Minh.

## HO CHI MINH

Ho Chi Minh is considered the George Washington of Vietnam. The Vietnamese look upon him as the founder of their country. He was born in 1890 in central Vietnam. He was originally named Nguyen Sinh Cung. The son of a minor government official and teacher, Ho received a good education at a French high school in Hue. He taught school briefly, then left Vietnam as a deckhand on a cargo ship and spent three years at sea.

Ho visited the United States at the age of twenty-three, seeing cities such as Boston and San Francisco. In New York City, he worked briefly in a restaurant kitchen. During this time, though, his thoughts were about Vietnam. He hated the fact that the

French ruled his country. They treated the Vietnamese as inferior beings and gave them only enough to keep them alive. The young man left the United States for Paris, France, where thousands of Vietnamese were living.

Ho changed his name to Nguyen Ai Quoc, which means Nguyen the Patriot. He produced revolutionary pamphlets and joined radical political groups. When World War I ended in 1918, he tried to focus world attention on French occupation of Vietnam as part of a world peace plan. But England, France, and the United States were more interested in solving European problems. The small, thin man who loved his country became involved with communism and went to Moscow in 1924 for a look at the new Communist government. He was impressed.

Ho wandered south out of Russia and into China. There he found little interest in Vietnam's plight. The Chinese were more worried about the rise of the Japanese. So Ho went to Bangkok, Thailand, and rallied Vietnamese living there. Ho traveled back and forth across Asia in the 1930s. He probably saw some of the terrible war inflicted on the Chinese countryside by the invading Japanese. Ho sneaked into Vietnam in 1941 and, with a few followers, decided to live in rural areas and make war against both the French and the Japanese. Ho and his revolutionaries wanted to rid their country of all foreign influence.

The rural guerrillas considered themselves allies of the United States during World War II. They rescued downed American pilots and hid them from Japanese soldiers. After the war, Ho and his followers marched into Hanoi and declared Vietnam independent. He based his independence on the United States Declaration of Independence and he asked for American aid. But the British convinced the United States that France should rule

Vietnam. So Ho returned to his jungle hideout as the French sailed into the harbor of Haiphong in 1946.

At this time, the entire section of Southeast Asia—Vietnam, Laos, and Cambodia—was known as French Indochina. Ho's band of guerrilla fighters recruited fellow Vietnamese. They used old weapons and homemade booby traps to ambush the French. Never healthy, Ho suffered from malaria and other diseases as he lived and worked in damp caves, hiding from the French. His courage served as a great example to his people. After the important battle at a town called Dien Bien Phu in 1954, the French agreed to leave Vietnam.

An agreement was made in Geneva, Switzerland, to split Vietnam in half. Ho and his fellow Communists felt they had earned the right to unite all of Vietnam. They watched as a rival government was set up in South Vietnam. Ho was elected president of the Democratic Republic of (North) Vietnam.

By 1965, Ho was in ill health. He became a symbol as much as he had ever been a leader. Ho died in 1969, while fighting still raged between North and South Vietnam. He had few possessions and no wife or children. In his will, he told the Vietnamese that "we are sure to win total victory."

## LE LOI

Next to Ho Chi Minh, Le Loi is Vietnam's greatest hero. He was born about A.D. 1400 and became a fisherman in what is now central Vietnam. Le Loi got his neighbors excited against the Chinese, who ruled the land at this time. They raised an army and, riding elephants, attacked the Chinese soldiers with bows and arrows and spears.

Like the guerrillas centuries later, his people attacked the Chinese only when they greatly outnumbered their enemies. In a crucial battle in 1426, Le Loi's forces routed the Chinese in a muddy field west of Hanoi. Two years later, a peace treaty was signed and the neighbors to the north withdrew.

Le Loi established a capital at Hanoi and became a king. He ruled well. He became interested in public works projects, helping build dams, dikes, and bridges for his people. By the year of his death, 1460, agricultural production had reached new records.

## THE TRUNG SISTERS

Not all famous Vietnamese are men. These women lived long ago, about the same time as Christ. They were named Trung Trac and Trung Nhi. The two rallied the Vietnamese against a cruel Chinese emperor after the emperor ordered Trung Trac's husband put to death. Within a few months, the army led by the women had freed sixty-five Vietnamese towns of Chinese rule. Vietnam was on the verge of complete independence.

The Chinese sent a huge army south into Vietnam. Battle after battle took place, and the sisters were in the thick of it. Gradually, the Chinese gained the upper hand because they had many more soldiers. The sisters committed suicide by jumping into a river.

## NGUYEN CAO KY

The Trung sisters prove that heroes and heroines don't always win. Such was the case with Nguyen Cao Ky, a South Vietnamese pilot and politician who remained in South Vietnam until the day northern forces overran Saigon.

Ky was born in northern Vietnam in 1930 and fought for the French against the Communists. He went south when the country was divided in 1954 and became South Vietnam's best fighter pilot. The Americans liked and admired him because he was always anxious to attack the enemy.

Ky got involved in politics. He and Nguyen Van Thieu came to power in 1965. They were quickly blamed by the people for unpopular policies. Ky became a foe of the South Vietnamese leaders and so returned to the air force. He left Vietnam in 1975 and today lives in California.

## VO NGUYEN GIAP

Giap perfected hit-and-run guerrilla tactics after World War II against the French. His Vietnamese Communist forces attacked the French in 1946 and were slaughtered. So Giap and his men ambushed, hid, sabotaged, and booby trapped. This longtime friend and student of Ho Chi Minh wore down the French and won an important battle in 1954 at Dien Bien Phu. The French then left Vietnam.

But Giap was then faced with overcoming South Vietnamese forces and their allies, the Americans. He relied on military hardware from Russia and China, combined with careful planning. His troops were among the very best in the world. Giap wasn't perfect—his ambush of the United States marines at Khe Sanh in 1968 did not work. But he was a master strategist.

A one-time law student and a teacher, Giap once told a reporter that he lost everything he cared about when his wife and infant son died in a French prison in 1941. Born in central Vietnam in 1912, Giap retired in 1981.

*A panoramic view of Ho Chi Minh City and a sidewalk market (inset)*

# Chapter 11

# *VISITING VIETNAM*

A trip to today's Vietnam is worth the experience, despite inconveniences. All visitors must be on a tour—there are no accommodations for people who want to explore. There are only two ways into the country and both of them are by air. Flights land in Ho Chi Minh City (formerly Saigon) and in Hanoi. The most common place to leave for Vietnam is Bangkok, though the Soviets and the French operate flights from their countries. There are no entry points for tourists at borders or at ports.

## CITIES OF THE SOUTH

Visitors who land in Ho Chi Minh City can see military planes in storage at what once was Tan Son Nhut Air Force Base. Transportation into the city may be an olive-drab school bus, another souvenir left by departing American servicemen. It has wire mesh to protect the windows, needs new parts, and does not run well on the poorly refined gasoline. Most taxis are parked and have not moved since 1975. Accommodations are likely to be in a

*A street scene (above) and the Botanical Gardens (right)*

splendid, old hotel constructed for nineteenth-century French travelers. The walls need paint and there may be tiny lizards walking the ceiling, but the rooms are clean.

Because there is now enough food for Vietnamese citizens, visitors can eat at small restaurants or in the hotel. The food mixes French and Chinese cooking and features locally grown tea or Vietnamese beer, but no foreign wine or familiar soft drinks. Much of wartime Saigon has vanished. No one begs on the streets or attempts to sell visitors freshly stolen watches or television sets. The black market exists, but it's hard to find—and it's being prodded by the government's new attitude toward a bit of private enterprise. Books, art, souvenirs, shoes, clothing, digital watches, pocket calculators, kitchen utensils, carryout food, tea, and fresh fruits and vegetables are sold in stalls and shops. People dress fairly well and seem relaxed.

*Rush hour in Ho Chi Minh City (left) and a young boy carrying a bird cage (right)*

One of the biggest changes is the lack of cars and, most of all, the lack of motorbikes. Thousands of small, smoke-spitting, Japanese cycles kept the air blue night and day in wartime Saigon. Some are still around, but bicycles are more common. Ho Chi Minh City supports itself with light industry, such as food processing, furniture making, and carpet weaving, plus retailing and civic projects. The city has about two million residents—half the size of old Saigon. With 80 percent of all southern Vietnamese engaged in farming, it appears to the visitor that the other 20 percent all live in Ho Chi Minh City.

Landmarks such as the exclusive Cercle Sportif club are now museums or have other public uses. Cholon, where Vietnamese of Chinese heritage once lived, now has far fewer Chinese. This district of narrow streets and shops, homes and factories shows that many ethnic Chinese have left the country. The city is much

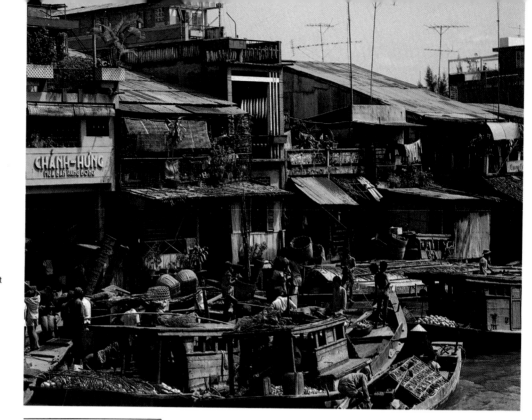

*Loading boats in My Tho*

quieter than before 1975, but it is also more disease ridden. The water in canals and in the Saigon River contains dangerous amounts of lead and is terribly polluted.

A side trip south to the Mekong Delta city of My Tho indicates that rice production has greatly improved. This largest of delta cities has been rebuilt and, like most other towns, has an active market. Fishing is a major activity here. My Tho became known worldwide during the war when a Vietnamese pilot accidentally dropped napalm on a Buddhist temple where civilians were hiding. A photo of a burned, naked little girl running down a road made the war real to newspaper readers everywhere. Happily, the girl, now an adult, has almost fully recovered from her wounds.

Two other southern cities need to be mentioned. Tay Ninh, west of Ho Chi Minh City, is the home of the Cao Dai religious sect. Their church is a wonderful, colorful mixture of every conceivable

*Left: Da Lat on the southern edge of the highlands*
*Right: The colorful Cao Dai temple in Tay Ninh*

style of religious art and architecture. Fortunately, the war missed this building, which looks like a Roman Catholic cathedral covered with dragons. The other city, Da Lat, is on the southern edge of the highlands. Wealthy Saigon residents used to seek relief from the heat here. They relaxed in handsome, European-style homes built by wealthy Frenchmen. Nowadays, Da Lat is an important site for growing exports such as flowers, ornamental pines, and such delicacies as strawberries.

## CITIES OF CENTRAL VIETNAM

All of the larger cities in central Vietnam are on the coast, and with good reason. Central Vietnam is where only a narrow plain separates the mountains from the South China Sea. In fact, the mountains actually meet the sea at a place named Hai Van Pass.

*Da Nang*

That's north of Da Nang, the site during the recent war of a huge
United States air base.

Today, Da Nang is large and busy, without much color. It is one
of the leading areas in Vietnam where scrap metal from the war is
being stockpiled for sale to the Japanese. Like most large
Vietnamese towns, few streets are paved. The rainy season can
turn any street into muddy soup. The area's major attraction is
nearby Marble Mountain, with its Confucian temple deep within.

In contrast to Da Nang is the romantic city of Hue, just a few
miles north along the coast. This ancient site was where Vietnam
kings and queens long ago held court. Though fighting here was
intense, the ancient citadel (a copy of China's Forbidden City) still
stands. There are many temples, palaces, and tombs to visit.
Across the lovely Perfume River flowing through the city are
lovely orchards. Some of Hue's Buddhist temples have
restaurants, gardens, and guides in saffron-colored robes, just for
visitors.

Top: Marble Mountain near Da Nang
The Royal Palace (left) and
royal tombs (above) in Hue

*Above: The beach at the resort town of Nha Trang*
*Below: The Ho Chi Minh Mausoleum in Hanoi*

*New construction on the Red River in Hanoi*

The central city farthest south is Nha Trang, a resort town with beautiful, clean beaches. Nearby is Cam Ranh Bay, where United States navy ships once unloaded troops and tons of cargo. Today, the port is the only Soviet naval base in the southwest Pacific. Nha Trang is a bit run-down, but has a wonderful park facing the sea where people do morning exercises. Between Nha Trang and Hue lie ruins of an ancient, Indian-based civilization known as the Chams.

## CITIES OF THE NORTH

Hanoi is the nation's capital. People have had less contact with foreigners and sometimes dress in drab military surplus-style clothing. The thousands of pale yellow, two-story shop houses now compete for attention with several newly built offices. There are several nice parks with lakes and the tomb of Ho Chi Minh is here. A few cottage industries are beginning. Families work together to make or sell tea, soup, cigarettes, bamboo mats, embroidered clothing, and other crafts. Women can be seen bent over manual sewing machines. Men and boys busy themselves with patches, glue, and air pumps to fix flat tires on the thousands of bicycles.

*In the city and the countryside, bicycles are common forms of transportation. Above: A pedicab driver waits for a fare.*

*The Hanoi market*

There is little evidence of the bombing that ended in 1972. In fact, the edges of the capital look almost prosperous, with Vietnamese showing their gardening ability. Also near Hanoi are cement works, cotton mills, an iron and steel complex, and an industrial park where items such as bicycles are made. These industries have been built or rebuilt with foreign aid, much of it Russian. Accurate figures are hard to obtain, but one set of figures shows how dependent the Vietnamese are on the Soviets. The gross national product is $20 billion. The Soviets must add $1 billion to that figure each year for Vietnam to get by.

## THE FUTURE

The economy remains agricultural and the heart of the country remains the village. Vietnamese tradition says the government can do what it wants, but that governmental authority ends at the village gate. That is more true today than in the recent past. New governmental bosses have found that a light touch makes people more productive and happier. Perhaps being sensitive to the needs of its citizens will result in fewer boat people and a better way of life for all Vietnamese.

## MAP KEY

| | | | | | |
|---|---|---|---|---|---|
| An Loc | G7 | Ha Dong | B6 | Phan Thiet | G8 |
| An Nhon | F8 | Ha Giang | A6 | Phu Cuong | G7 |
| An Tuc | F8 | Ha Tien | G6 | Phu Quoc (island) | G5, G6 |
| Annam (region) | D7 | Ha Tinh | C6 | Phu Tho | B6 |
| Ba Don | D7 | Hai Duong | B7 | Phu Vinh | H7 |
| Bac Can | A6 | Haiphong | B7 | Phuoc Le | G7 |
| Bac Ninh | B7 | Ham Tan | G7 | Plain of Reeds | G6, G7 |
| Bac Quang | A6 | Hanoi | B6 | Pleiku | F7 |
| Bach Long VI (island) | B7 | Hao Binh | B6 | Quan Long | H6 |
| Baie de Ben Goi | F8 | Ho Chi Minh City (Saigon) | G7 | Quang Ngai | E8 |
| Ban Me Thuot | F8 | Hoai Nhon | E8 | Quang Tri | D7 |
| Bao Ha | A6 | Hoi An | E8 | Qui Nhon | F8 |
| Bien Hoa | G7 | Hoi Xuan | B6 | Rach Gia | G6 |
| Black River | B5, B6 | Hon Gai | B7 | Red River | B6 |
| Ca River | C6 | Hue | D7 | Ron | D7 |
| Cai Bau (island) | B7 | Iles Kao Tao (islands) | B7 | Sapatu (island) | H8 |
| Cam Pha | B7 | Iles de Poulo Dama (islands) | H6 | Son La | B5 |
| Can Tho | G6 | Khanh Hung | H6 | Son Tay | B6 |
| Cao Bang | A7 | Khoai (island) | H6 | Song Cau | F8 |
| Cat Ba (island) | B7 | Kontum | E8 | Tam Ky | E8 |
| Chau Phu | G6 | Lai Chau | A5 | Tan An | G7 |
| Cheo Reo | F8 | Lang Son | B7 | Tay Ninh | G7 |
| Chuoi (island) | H6 | Lao Cai | A6 | Thai Binh | B7 |
| Cochin China (region) | G7 | Lay (cape) | D7 | Thai Nguyen | B6 |
| Con Son (island) | H7 | Linh (mountain) | E7 | Thanh Hoa | C6 |
| Cu Lao (island) | G8 | Loc Ninh | G7 | Tien Yen | B7 |
| Cu Lao Cham (island) | E8 | Long Xuyen | G6 | To Bong | F8 |
| Cu Lao Re (island) | E8 | Me (island) | C6 | Tonkin (region) | B6 |
| Da Lat | G8 | Moc Hoa | G6 | Truc Giang | G7 |
| Da Nang | D8 | Mouths of the Mekong (delta) | H7 | Tuy Hoa | F8 |
| Deux Freres (island) | H7 | Mui Bai Bung (island) | H6 | Tuyen Quang | B6 |
| Di Linh | G8 | Mui Dieu (island) | F8 | Vinh | C6 |
| Dien Bien Phu | B5 | Mui Ron (island) | C7 | Vinh Cam Ranh | G8 |
| Dinh Lap | B7 | Mui Vung Tau (island) | G7 | Vinh Loi | H6 |
| Dong Hoi | D7 | My Tho | G7 | Vinh Long | G6 |
| Duong Dong | G5 | Na Sam | A7 | Vinh Yen | B6 |
| Fan Si Pan (mountain) | A5 | Nam Dinh | B7 | Vong Phu (mountain) | F8 |
| Gia Dinh | G7 | Nha Trang | F8 | Way (island) | H5 |
| Gio (island) | D7 | Ninh Binh | B6 | Xuan Loc | G7 |
| Grande Catwick (island) | G8 | Panjang (island) | H5 | Xuy Nong Chao (island) | B7 |
| Gulf of Tonkin | C7 | Phan Rang | G8 | Yang Sin (mountain) | F8 |
| | | | | Yen Bay | B6 |

112

3 100° 4 102° 5 104° 6 106° 7 108° 8 110° 9

CHINA

A

Takut
Lancang
Simao
Menglian
Menghai
Muang Ou Nua
Hokou
Lao Cai
Bao Ha
Ha Giang
Cao Bang
Nanning
Hengxian
Yulin (Waitlam)
Luchuan
Luoding
FAN-SI-PAN 10312
Lai Chau
Bac Quang
Bac Kan
Na Sam
Pinghsiang
Longzhou
Fusui (Funan)
Ningming Suilu
GUANG-DONG

Takaw
Keng Tung
Jinghong (Yunjinghong)
Muang Ou Tai
Phongsali
Son La
Dien Bien Phu
Tuyen Quang
Yen Bai
Thai Nguyen
Lang Son
Dinh Lap
Tien Yen
Dongxing
Beihai
WEIZHOU DAO
Qinzhou
Lianjiang
Maoming
Dianbai (Tinpak)
Wuchuan (Meilü)

B

Mong Hsat
Muang Sing
Louang Namtha
Phu Tho
Vinh Yen
Bac Ninh
Hon Gay
Cam Pha
Zhanjiang (Tsamkong)
Haikang (Hoihong)
Xuwen

Hanoi
Ha Dong
Hai Duong
Haiphong
CAT BA
LUICHOW PEN.

Chiang Khong
Fang
Chiang Rai
Chiang Kham
Xam Nua
Nam Dinh
Thai Binh
XUY NONG CHAO
Lingao
Xinzhou
Chengmai
Haikou (Hoihow)

CHIANG DAO

Hoi Xuan
Ninh Binh
BACH LONG VI
Danxian (Nada)
Qiongshan

20°

Son
Chiang Mai
Lamphun
Lampang
Nan
Louangphrabang
PLATEAU DU TRANNINH
Muang Lan
Thanh Hoa
ME
HAINAN (CHINA)
Beili
Dongfang (Basuo)
WUZHI SHAN 6125
Baoting
Wenchang (Mencheong)

C

Muang Souy
Xiangkhoang
BIA 9252
Muang Pakxan
LOI 7405
Gancheng
Yacheng
Yaxian (Sanya)
Yülin

Phrae
Nan
Muang Xaignabouri
Vinh
Nape
Ha Tinh
C. RON MA

18°

Uttaradit
Viangchan
Nong Khai
Ron
Ba Don
Dong Hoi
CON CO
C. LAY

D

Sawankhalok
Sukhothai
Tak
Loei
Udon Thani
Muang Khammouan
Quang Tri

Phitsanulok
Phichit
Lom Sak
Sakon Nakhon
Muang Xepon
Hue
Da Nang
CHAM

Kamphaeng Phet
Phetchabun
Khon Kaen
Kalasin
Savannakhet

MOKOCHU 6444

16°

Nakhon Sawan
Uthai Thani
Chainat
Maha Sarakham
Roi Et
Yasothon
Khemmarat
Saravan
Muang Khongxedon
Pakse
Hoi An
Tam Ky
Quang Ngai
RE
NAM

THAILAND (SIAM)

E

Lop Buri
Phutthaisong
Ubon Ratchathani
PLATEAU DES BOLOVENS
LINH 8524
Attapu
Hoai Nhon
Kontum

Nakhon Ratchasima
Buriram
Sisaket
Campasak

Suphan Buri
Nam Tok
Kanchanaburi
Nakhon Pathom
Sara Buri
KHIEO 4357
Nang Rong
Khu Khan
DONGRAK
Muang Khong
Virochey
Pleiku
An Tuc
An Nhon
Qui Nhon
Song Cau

14°

PHANOM
Phumi Samraong

Bangkok
Krung Thep
Chachoengsao
Prachin Buri
Sa Kaeo
Paoy Pet
ANGKOR
Stoeng Treng
Hau Bon
Tuy Hoa
C. KE GA

RAT Buri
Samut Sakhon
SI CHANG
Chon Buri
Aranyaprathet
Siemreab
Kampong Thum
Buon Me Thuot
VONG PHU 6634

F

Phet Buri
KHRAM YAI
Rayong
Batdambang
Kampong Khleang
Kracheh
YANG SIN 7890
Nha Trang
Da Lat

KAMPUCHEA (CAMBODIA)

12°

Mergui
Pran Buri
Sattahip
Chanthaburi
Trat
CHANG
Pouthisat
Kampong Thum
Loc Ninh
An Loc
Phan Rang
Cam Ranh

Tenasserim
Kampong Chhnang
AORAL 5810
Kampong Cham
An Loc
Di Linh
Cam Ranh Bay

Prachuap Khiri Khan
KUT
Phnom Penh
Prey Veng
Tay Ninh
Phu Cuong
Bien Hoa
Phan Thiet

Bang Saphan
KONG
Kampong Spoe
Svay Rieng
Gia Dinh
Ho Chi Minh City (Saigon)
Vung Tau
Ham Tan

G

Chumphon
ISTHMUS OF KRA
TAO
RUNG
Takev
Chau Phu
Moc Hoa
PLAIN OF REEDS
Loc Ninh
C. VUNG TAU
THU
ILES CATWICK

PHANGAN
SAMUI
Kampong Saom (Sihanoukville)
Duong Dong
PHU QUOC
Ha Tien
Kampot
Long Xuyen
My Tho
Tan An
Truc Giang
Vinh Long

10°

Thani
Thung Song
WAI IS.
Rach Gia
Can Tho
Phu Vinh
Quan Long

a Pa
NAM DU IS.
THO CHU
Khanh Hung
Mouths of the Mekong

H

Nakhon Si Thammarat
MALAY
Quan Long
Bac Lieu
CON SON
DEUX FRÈRES

CHUOI
C. CA MAU
KHOAI

8°

Phatthalung
Trang
Kantang
Songkhla
Hat Yai

Cosmopolitan World Atlas, © Copyright 1989 by Rand McNally & Company,
R.L. 88-S-147

I

Gulf of Tonkin
Hainan
South China Sea
Gulf of Thailand
LAOS
VIET-NAM

# MINI-FACTS AT A GLANCE

## GENERAL INFORMATION

**Official Name:** The Socialist Republic of Vietnam (*Cong Hoa Xa Hoi Chu Nghia Viet Nam*)

**Capital:** Hanoi

**Official Language:** Vietnamese

**Government:** Governmental practice reflects Chinese Communist principles. A resolution of the North Vietnamese National Assembly in December 1975 and a decree by the Provisional Revolutionary Government in the South in February 1976 reorganized the country into 35 provinces, each run by a people's council. In April 1976, elections were held for a new National Assembly.

The assembly proclaimed the unificiation of Vietnam as the Socialist Republic of Vietnam. The constitution states that the National Assembly is the supreme organ of the government. The Council of Ministers is comprised of the prime minister and deputy prime ministers, all of whom are named by the assembly, and the heads of government ministries and various state organizations. However, the most important political institution is the Vietnamese Communist party. The chairman of the Party is the most powerful political leader of the country. Any citizen of 18 or over "who has engaged in labor and has not been an exploiter" is eligible to join.

**National Song:** "Tien Quan a" ("Hymn of the Marching Army")

**Flag:** The flag and coat of arms both feature a star that stands for communism. The large yellow star is centered on a red background. The rice and the cogwheel on the coat of arms represent the importance of agriculture and industry. The flag was adopted by North Vietnam in 1955.

**Money:** The basic unit of currency is the dong. In the summer of 1988, 80 dong were worth 1 U.S. dollar.

**Weights and Measures:** Vietnam uses the metric system.

**Population:** Estimated 1988 population—62,996,000; 80 percent rural, 20 percent urban

**Major Cities**
| | |
|---|---:|
| Ho Chi Minh City | 3,460,000 |
| Hanoi | 1,443,500 |
| Haiphong | 1,190,900 |

(Population based on 1976 census)

**Religion:** Most Vietnamese are Buddhists, but the beliefs of Taoism and Confucianism shape the Vietnamese world view.

Roman Catholicism was first introduced in the seventeenth century, and it spread widely with the French conquest in the mid-nineteenth century. Though the 1960 constitution guaranteed freedom of religion, the North Vietnamese government tried to gain control by sponsoring patriotic religious organizations. These included the Unified Buddhist church, the Patriotic Catholic church, the Viet Nam Cao Dai Union, and the Vietnam Protestant church.

## GEOGRAPHY

**Highest Point:** Fan Si Pan, 10,312 ft. (3,143 m), above sea level

**Lowest Point:** Sea level along the coast

**Mountains:** The Annamite Cordillera is a range of mountains and highlands that stretches from eastern Tibet and Yunnan in China to within a few miles of Saigon and the Mekong River delta.

The Northern Highlands are a mountainous region in northwestern Vietnam. They extend into China and Laos.

**Rivers:** The Red River flows northwest to southeast from its source in Yunnan. The Vietnamese portion is about 725 mi. (1,166 km) long.

The Mekong River, which originates in Tibet, terminates in southern Vietnam. The rivers are major highways.

**Climate:** Vietnam has a tropical monsoon type of climate, with hot, wet summers and mild, dry winters. The interior highlands have drier winters and cooler year-round temperatures than the lowland areas. At Ho Chi Minh City, typical of the southern lowlands, the average summer temperature is 85° F. (29.4° C), and the average winter temperature is 78° F. (25.6° C). The comparable range for Hanoi, typical of the northern lowlands, is 85° F. (29.4° C) in summer and 62° F. (16.7° C) in winter.

The rainfall varies from year to year. Almost all of Ho Chi Minh City's annual rainfall of about 80 in. (203 cm) occurs between April and October. Hue receives about 116 in. (294 cm), much of it in the fall and winter from the northeast winter monsoons.

**Greatest Distances:** North to south—1,030 mi. (1,657 km)
East to west—380 mi. (612 km)
Coastline—2,038 mi. (3,280 km)

**Area:** 127,242 sq. mi. (329,556 km²)

# NATURE

**Trees:** Evergreen forests include conifers and deciduous trees. There are more than 1,500 species of woody plants, varying in size from small shrubs to large trees and ranging from hardwoods such as ebony and teak to palms, mangroves, and bamboo. Rain forests are relatively limited.

During the Vietnam War, herbicides were used by the U.S. army to defoliate forests in South Vietnam. About one-fifth of the total acreage was sprayed with chemicals that affected all types of vegetation.

**Animals:** The most common domesticated animals are water buffalo, cattle, dogs, cats, pigs, goats, ducks, and chickens. The largest wild animal is the elephant. There are also wild oxen, wild pigs, tapirs, tigers, leopards, and bears. Deer are plentiful. Porcupines, jackals, otters, mongooses, hares, and skunks are also abundant. Rats and mice are everywhere.

**Fish:** The principal fish to be found are species of tilapia, carp, catfish, and snakehead. Shellfish include lobster, shrimp, crab, and squid.

**Birds:** There are about 586 different kinds of birds in southern Vietnam alone.

# EVERYDAY LIFE

**Food:** The Vietnam diet is not unlike the diet of the Chinese. However, it is based on the foods that are grown in Vietnam: rice (the largest crop), sweet potatoes, corn, fish, and shellfish. The fish is often dried, since there is no refrigeration, or it is served with rice as *nuoc mam*, a fermented sauce that has a strong odor but a mild taste.

*Pho*, a hot soup made of noodles and onions with bits of beef in it, is also a staple of the Vietnamese diet. Tiny meatballs are popular.

Hot tea accompanies most meals.

Vendors sell noodles in many varieties.

**Housing:** Differences in climate influence the housing styles in northern and southern Vietnam. In the cooler north, wood or simple bamboo houses with tile roofs are common. In the south, palm leaves or straw are used in rural areas.

Highland people prefer to build their houses on pilings. Floor plans vary depending on whether the house will be occupied by an extended family and whether there are cultural proscriptions for part of the house. The Rhade people in the central highlands, for example, have young people live with their wives' families after marriage.

In the country today, sheets of metal or plastic are often used for roofs. Wood, brick, and tile are used in the modern towns and cities.

**Holidays:**

> January 1, New Year's Day, a festival lasting several days
> January 27, Vietnam Day, anniversary of peace agreements terminating
> Vietnam War, 1973
> February 3, founding date of Lao Dong party
> March 29, Vietnam Veterans Day, anniversary of withdrawal of American
> forces, 1973
> May 7, anniversary of Dien Bien Phu victory in 1954
> July 28, war invalids' Day
> August 19, Viet Minh insurrection in Hanoi in 1945
> September 2, celebrating establishment of Democratic Republic of Vietnam,
> 1949
> November 13, dedication of Vietnam Veterans Memorial in Washington,
> D.C., 1983
> December 19, anti-French resistance war begun in 1946
> December 22, founding of North Vietnamese army in 1944
> December 28, founding of National Front for Liberation of South Vietnam in
> 1960

**Culture:** The Chinese influence dominates Vietnamese culture, and it is evident in language, art, literature, music, theater, and architecture. Poetry is deeply rooted in the oral tradition and it was expressed in Chinese form and style.

The best-known Vietnamese poem is *Kim Van Kieu (The Tale of Kieu)* by Nguyen Du. It is an epic poem about a girl's struggle to maintain the honor of her family.

The French conquest also had a strong cultural impact. French literature is known to everyone who has a high-school diploma, and books written in French are available at street-corner stalls.

Traditional Chinese opera is popular. The theater is strictly controlled by the state. *Cai luong*, a satirical musical comedy, is often performed.

Painting is confined to socialist realism; it has failed to flourish. However, high-quality lacquer ware continues to be produced. Block prints are for sale all over the country.

In the highlands women weave blankets, skirts, blouses, and loincloths, and men weave baskets and mats.

There is a wide variety of musical instruments, but gongs are the most common. Vietnamese music is poetry that is sung.

**Communication:** Before the 1960s few Vietnamese owned a radio or a TV set. Such is still the case in northern Vietnam, but in southern Vietnam radios—and, to a lesser extent, TVs—have become prevalent. Most rural people live in villages and listen to radio programs in groups. TV sets are largely owned by collective farms, workers' organizations, and similar groups.

The Communist party has control over all means of communication.

**Transportation:** The geography of Vietnam has rendered transportation between the north and the south difficult. Except for air and sea, traffic has been limited to a narrow corridor along the coast. The two large deltas have good internal transportation systems based on vast networks of inland waterways, roads, and cart trails. Most coastal and ocean shipping is centered in the northern port of Haiphong and the southern port of Ho Chi Minh City.

The rail system suffered heavy damage during the war years.

Air travel is being developed. Noi Bai airport at Hanoi was opened to international traffic in 1978. Soviet, East German, Chinese, and Laotian aircraft use the facility.

The bicycle is the favorite method of transportation in Vietnam. Motor scooters are also popular. Less than 1 percent of the people own an automobile.

**Schools:** Education always has been important to the Vietnamese because of their Confucianist tradition. Rural education in the south was badly disrupted during the war years, and all schools were nationalized in 1975. The government pursued a policy of educational reform. Twelve years of schooling are provided free.

The government claims that illiteracy has been abolished in the south as it already had been in the north. Emphasis has been placed on training in science and technology. Several thousand students are sent abroad for study—some to Eastern Europe and the Soviet Union, but some also go to France, Great Britain, and Australia.

There are two universities and over forty colleges and specialty schools. The University of Ho Chi Minh City is the largest school of higher education.

**Health and Welfare:** After reunification, there was a general increase in health facilities and personnel throughout Vietnam. Health facilities include hospitals, health centers, sanatoriums, leprosy centers, and village health and maternity centers.

# ECONOMY AND INDUSTRY

### Principal Products:
*Agriculture:* rice
*Manufacturing:* cement, fertilizer, iron and steel, paper products, textiles
*Mining:* coal

# IMPORTANT DATES

1500 B.C.—Indonesians found kingdom of Champa on east coast

111 B.C.—The Chinese conquer what is now northern Vietnam

A.D. 40—Trung sisters lead revolt against China

939—The Chinese end their rule over the Vietnamese, who set up an independent state

1500—Portuguese sailors arrive

1600s—French missionaries arrive in Vietnam

1802—Nguyen Anh becomes emperor and unites the country and calls it Vietnam

1858-83—France takes control of Vietnam

1887—France creates Indochinese Union composed of Cochinchina, Annam, Tonkin, and Cambodia

1940-45—Japan controls Vietnam during World War II

1945—Ho Chi Mihn proclaims independence of Vietnam

1946—French return to Vietnam

1954—The Vietminh defeat the French; the Geneva Conference divides Vietnam into two areas separated by a provisional demarcation line

1957—The Viet Cong begin insurgency against the South Vietnamese; the Vietnam War develops

1960—North Vietnamese soldiers take Ho Chi Minh Trail to aid Viet Cong

1963—Buddhist monk sets himself afire

1964—U.S. Congress passes the Tonkin Gulf Resolution, which gives the president power to "take necessary measures to prevent future aggression." United States begins bombing of North Vietnam

1965—U.S. President Johnson sends marines into Da Nang

1968—Tet offensive; North Vietnamese and Viet Cong attack South Vietnamese cities and towns

1969—My Lai massacre announced; U.S. President Nixon says that U.S. troops would begin withdrawal from Vietnam; Ho Chi Minh dies at age 79

1973—The United States, North and South Vietnam, and the Viet Cong sign a cease-fire agreement; the last U.S. ground troops leave Vietnam

1975—South Vietnam surrenders after North Vietnamese capture Saigon

1976—Communists unify North and South Vietnam into the nation of Vietnam

1979—New constitution is adopted; China invades Vietnam

1986-87—Shakeup in government, Politburo comes under the control of a more pragmatic factor in order to strengthen the failed economy

## IMPORTANT PEOPLE

Bao Dai (1913-　), last emperor of Vietnam; puppet of the French; headed the government from 1949 to 1955

Ho Chi Minh (1890-1969), the George Washington of Vietnam; president of North Vietnam from 1945 to 1969

Lao-tzu (6th century B.C.), philosopher founder of Taoism

Le Duc Tho (1911-　), helped found Viet Minh; served as special adviser to North Vietnamese delegation to Paris Peace Conference (1968-73); nominated for 1973 Nobel Peace prize, but declined honor

Nguyen Cao Ky (1930-　), South Vietnamese pilot; vice-president of South Vietnam from 1965 to 1971

Ngo Dinh Diem (1901-63), prime minister of South Vietnam from 1954 to 1956; president until 1963 when he was assassinated

Nguyen Du (1765-1820), poet who wrote *Kim Van Kieu*

Nguyen Van Linh, general secretary of Vietnamese Communist party

Nguyen Van Thieu (1923-　), Ho Chi Minh's guerrilla leader; president of South Vietnam from 1967 to 1975

Nhu, Madame, wife of Ngo Dinh Nhu (brother of Ngo Dinh Diem); acted as South Vietnam's first lady from 1954 to 1963

Trung sisters, Trung Trac and Trung Nhi (?-A.D. 43), rallied the Vietnamese against a cruel Chinese emperor

Vo Nguyen Giap (1912-　), master military strategist; won battle of Dien Bien Phu against French in 1954

# INDEX

Page numbers that appear in boldface type indicate illustrations

## About the Author

David Wright was born on January 10, 1943, in Richmond, Indiana. He grew up in and around Richmond, graduating from high school in 1961. After he was graduated from Wittenberg University, Springfield, Ohio, in 1966, he was drafted and served two years in the United States army; one of the two years was spent in Vietnam. Wright has spent more than ten years in newspapers as a reporter, copy editor, and editor. Newspapers range from *The Chicago Tribune* to *The Monroe* (Wisconsin) *Times.*

Wright has written one book for adults, *The Harley-Davidson Motor Company*, and has edited three children's books. He has about one hundred magazine articles to his credit on subjects ranging from vending machines to travel by motorcycle. In this same series, he has written *Enchantment of the World: Malaysia.*

Wright and his wife and two children live in West Bend, Wisconsin, an hour northwest of Milwaukee. His hobbies include hiking, traveling, fishing, reading, and writing. He has been a full-time free-lance writer, editor, and photographer for ten years.

## DATE DUE

| | | | |
|---|---|---|---|
| | | | |
| | | | |
| | | | |
| | | | |
| | | | |
| | | | |
| | | | |
| | | | |
| | | | |
| | | | |
| | | | |
| | | | |